A Ragged Mountain Press
WOMAN'S GUIDE

SKIING

MAGGIE LORING

Series Editor, Molly Mulhern Gross

RAGGED MOUNTAIN PRESS / McGRAW-HILL

Camden, Maine • New York • San Francisco • Washington, D.C. • Auckland • Bogotá
Caracas • Lisbon • London • Madrid • Mexico City • Milan • Montreal
New Delhi • San Juan • Singapore • Sydney • Tokyo • Toronto

Look for these other Ragged Mountain Press Woman's Guides

Backpacking, Adrienne Hall
Canoeing, Laurie Gullion
Climbing, Shelley Presson
Fly-Fishing, Dana Rikimaru
Mountaineering, Andrea Gabbard

Powerboating, Sandy Lindsey
Sailing, Doris Colgate
Scuba Diving, Claire Walter
Sea Kayaking, Shelley Johnson
Snowboarding, Julia Carlson

Winter Sports, Iseult Devlin

• •

Ragged Mountain Press

A Division of The **McGraw·Hill** *Companies*

10 9 8 7 6 5 4 3 2 1

Library of Congress Cataloging-in-Publication Data
Loring, Maggie.
   Skiing / Maggie Loring.
      p.   cm. — (A Ragged Mountain Press woman's guide)
   Includes bibliographical references (p.) and index.
   ISBN 0-07-038867-9 (alk. paper)
   1. Skiing for women. I. Title. II. Series.
  GV854.34.L67   1999
  796.93'082—dc21
                           99-32853
                            CIP

Questions regarding the content of this book
should be addressed to
  Ragged Mountain Press
  P.O. Box 220, Camden, ME 04843
  http://www.raggedmountainpress.com

Questions regarding the ordering of this book
should be addressed to
  The McGraw-Hill Companies
  Customer Service Department
  P.O. Box 547, Blacklick, OH 43004
  Retail customers: 1-800-262-4729
  Bookstores: 1-800-722-4726

Printed by Quebecor Printing Company, Fairfield, PA
Edited by Patricia Sterling
Design by Carol Inouye, Inkstone Communications Design
Project management by Janet Robbins
Page layout by Shannon Thomas
Illustrations by Elayne Sears

Photographs by Dennis Curran except for the following: page 114, courtesy Allsport; page 83, courtesy Todd Powell/Mira; pages 33 (bottom), 34 (right), and 93 (bottom), courtesy Rossignol; page 119, courtesy Carver Girls/Sport Obermeyer/Biege Jones; pages 23 and 70, courtesy Tony Stone Images; and pages 13 and 112, courtesy Weststock.

A Ragged Mountain Press
WOMAN'S GUIDE

 **SKIING**

•••••••••••••••••••••••••••••••••

The best part about skiing is that
the adventure never stops.

•••••••••••••••••••••••••••••••••

Foreword

There's a small ski hill in my town. It's open as soon as the temperature drops below freezing, and it stays open until the maple sap runs in spring. On weekends the A-frame lodge buzzes with families chatting and ski boots clumping along the wooden floor. I go there whenever I can, for a long lunch or to help my four-year old practice his wedge turn. Everytime I go I see more and more women, some veterans of the slope, but many there for the very first time.

A newcomer once stopped me at the top of an intermediate slope. Abandoned by her skiing "buddies" and near tears, she just wanted off the mountain. I did what I could to calm her, conveyed the basics of the wedge position (see pages 45–46), and escorted her back to the lodge. She learned the hard way how *not* to head up the mountain: without a lesson. When I see such obviously uncomfortable beginners on the slope, I wonder if they'll ever try skiing again. I hope they won't miss learning a lifelong sport just because their friends didn't know any better. This book is designed to prevent just that kind of traumatic start. Maggie takes you through all the right steps involved in learning to ski. She'll demystify the rental process and explain what to expect in your first lesson. She'll even let you know where to park your car. By following her advice and suggestions we're hoping that you enjoy your first experiences, and come back to the slopes many a time.

Why a book on skiing for women? You might welcome a different approach, one that includes the voices of others who are also learning a new sport. Gear, clothing, and certain issues—like our ability to admit that we're scared to death to ride the chairlift—are just different for us. Not to mention that it's fun to learn with like-minded folk. So let Maggie introduce you to the world of the female skier. In this book she'll teach you how to dress so you can ski all day without getting cold, find boots and skis made with the woman skier in mind, and find women's-only ski weekends.

What's so different about the way women learn? If you're like me, you want to hear a description of a method or tactic before launching into it. I'm a fan of the talk-it-over-and-think-it-through-first school of learning. I prefer to ask questions *before* I'm asked to swing myself onto a chairlift. I want to hear advice from someone who thinks like I do. And I like to learn in a group so I can hear other folks' questions—and know I'm not the only one wondering how to tell my left ski from the right (there's no difference, see page 44).

We've done our best to mimic the learning conditions of a woman's instructional clinic in The Ragged Mountain Press Woman's Guides. There's a sense of camaraderie, honesty, and just plain fun. Here you'll find lots of women's voices: your instructor's, of course, but also voices of women from all walks who love the outdoors. *Skiing: A Woman's Guide* provides solutions, advice, and stories from women who have done what you are about to do: learn to ski. I hope Maggie's words and approach help get you out exploring and enjoying, by yourself or with a friend. I'll look for you out there.

Between ski trips, drop us a note to tell us how we're doing and how we can improve these guides to best suit you and your learning style.

MOLLY MULHERN GROSS
Series Editor, The Ragged Mountain Press Woman's Guides
Camden, Maine
August 1999

An avid outdoorswoman, Molly Mulhern Gross enjoys running, hiking, camping, sea kayaking, telemark skiing, in-line skating, biking, and snowboarding. She is Director of Editing, Design, and Production at Ragged Mountain Press and International Marine.

CONTENTS

CONTENTS

Acknowledgments

This book features the expertise of many people. I hope it provides a straightforward look at the sport we all love and inspires women who have not yet experienced the thrill of skiing. Special thanks to those women who continue to pioneer in a male-dominated sport: Carol Levine, Dee Byrne, Mermer Blakeslee (my mentors and friends), and others who have added to the direction for women in skiing, Claudia Carbone, and Jeannie Thoren to name just a couple.

I also thank Elan Skis and especially Mike (Gootz) Getzinger and Bill Irwin for providing me with many skis to test and for accepting my input for developing skis for women and children.

A special thank-you is in order for Mimi Philbrick and her daughter Tera for posing for many photographs, even when some depicted them as less than perfect! They took falls and kept on filming with grace and dignity even when the skies opened up during the bump run.

Thanks to my daughter Karin, who found the perfect children to photograph, patiently went shopping, and kept me laughing through a very long day of photos.

This book would not be possible without the inspiration of Molly Mulhern Gross, the brainchild for the whole series, and the support team at Ragged Mountain Press, who patiently whipped my ramblings and hen-scratch into shape.

Ultimately, *none* of this would be possible if my parents had not spent the time and energy to bring our family of nine skiing every weekend for as long as I can remember. Thanks for letting me skip school sometimes, Dad, and Mom, thanks for making the lunches and wiping my tears when I didn't win races. I love you both.

Thanks to my adoring husband for patiently listening to passages from the manuscript night after night, and for telling me when it was time to quit and get some sleep. You are my soul mate . . . I hope we ski together forever!

Finally, thanks to Judy, Kim, Jan, Beverly, and the other women who appear throughout the pages of this book. Without your time and willingness to share, the future of women in sport would be much less exciting!

Chapter 1

SKIING: A WOMAN'S PERSPECTIVE

Children need to feel good about something. I felt good about skiing. From the moment my dad took me skiing at age five, I was a star. I still remember my excitement when he brought home my white wooden skis and lace-up boots. With my "big kid" desire, I knew I was going to do something very special.

The key is preparation, practice, and enjoying every step of the way.

My four brothers and two sisters and I took part in a weekly children's ski program. My first teachers were a husband and wife team named Phyllis and Earl. Phyllis wore fuzzy fur hats, had a gruff voice, and was full of encouragement. With her help, I learned to ski by myself right away. I remember the adults were amazed at how quickly I learned.

Later I took private lessons with Phyllis and sometimes with Earl—my hero—who could make skiing look like dancing. I secretly wanted to be a ballerina, and they left no doubt that I too would be able to dance on skis.

I competed in a program called Junior Masters, designed for skiers who didn't want to race. It later became what is now known as freestyle. Back then we performed compulsory maneuvers (like ice skaters' school figures) and two free skiing runs, one designed to be smooth and flowing, the other active and exciting. At age twelve I competed in a New England regional event and had the skiing experience that changed my life and earned me a spot on the Eastern Junior

Demonstration Team. I felt my first true carved turn! I'll never forget the feeling of my skis slicing through the snow in a perfect arc. It was a "flow" experience that I wanted to repeat again and again—very exciting for a young girl. From that moment I've dedicated myself to helping others get that same feeling of connection to the snow.

When you know how to prepare and what to expect, skiing can provide recreation, fitness, and magical experiences in the winter outdoors. This book can help you start your adventure successfully.

THE EXPERIENCE OF SKIING: BODY, MIND, SPIRIT

Though it may seem like a mindless free fall down the face of a mountain, skiing takes critical thinking. The skier's mind and body must connect to perform appropriate movements, processing external and internal information simultaneously. The continual decisions about speed, direction, and intensity of movements can be both challenging and stimulating. This total involvement in the moment can offer respite from normal thoughts and daily routines and provide a new perspective.

When properly taught, a woman of advancing years can move down the mountain as effortlessly as a young girl, a self-professed nonathlete can evoke new responses from her body, and a sportswoman can explore new movements and sensations. In one day, given the right coaching, conditions, and logistics, you should be able to connect turns on the learning slope. In a week's time you'll be exploring the mountain. Of course there are trails and runs that are fun only for more advanced skiers, but you'll be able to cover enough acreage to provide a true skiing adventure. At the other extreme, there's no "end" to learning to ski. Even those of us who have been skiing for over thirty years continue to grow and learn and to have rewarding new sensations and experiences.

Skiing can be an outlet for expression of self and an opportunity to share crisp winter

moments with others. You can practice it alone, honing your skills minute to minute and turn to turn, or you can simply feel the delight of gliding down the mountain's shoulder, in control and exhilarated by the wind on your face and your companion's tracks ahead. Whereas men often challenge each other to ski faster or jump higher, women tend to let others experience their own thrill and to support each other in pursuit of it.

Skiing allows you to explore mountains in the winter, experience the many facets of snow surfaces, and discover new responses from skis collaborating with the snow. You can be in the company of friends yet meet an individual challenge. You can escape your day-to-day grind and

The author "making tracks."

float freely through a white expanse where there are no judgments but your tracks.

SKIERS I'VE KNOWN

Women who ski are as varied as any group of women. They range in age from three to ninety-three and run the gamut from slender to stocky, slight to strong, solitary to social, and shy to self-assured. Some women ski to get outside in the wintertime, some use skiing as a social outlet. Some started as children and want to recreate lasting memories for their own families. Some are grandmothers spending time with grandchildren. Whatever their reasons, women ski to enjoy the winter and savor the extremes of skiing: cold snow to warm fire, crisp, clear breeze to cozy lodge.

Skiing is a social sport. Here the author cranks a few turns with friend Mimi Philbrick.

A cure for cabin fever

My teenage friend Jan spends summers hiking and writing poetry, and skiing gets her outside in the winter as well. Jan learned to ski as a small child, encouraged by her dad, who also skied. On the high-school race team she met friendly competition on the slopes and had many adventures with her friends.

As Jan entered adolescence, her parents found they had little in common with their moody, creative daughter. Yet skiing still offered them exciting vacations and family time. "It's really brought me closer to my dad," explains Jan. "We take special trips and have special days just to ski together." Jan will be off to college soon but is already looking forward to skiing as a way to enjoy the outdoors with new friends.

Adventures with friends

Judy began skiing to be with her boyfriend. She wanted to be outside in the winter and was also looking for adventure with friends. She learned to ski along with her cousin, and both married professional ski teachers. Judy reflects nostalgically on the weekends spent at the ski resort: "We'd ski all day and play all night! It was such a great way to meet new people and enjoy the winter." Now Judy is a bank executive, an independent career woman with a family. She continues to take advantage of new opportunities at the ski resort to relax, meet new friends, and escape the daily grind.

Family time

Kim, a nurse practitioner, learned to ski in middle school. In college she skied as a social occasion and to break the monotony of her studies. Afterward Kim traveled around the country as part of a nursing corps. Her love for skiing brought her many chances to meet people and find recreation in the mountains. Now, with three active children approaching their teens and a husband who is equally outdoorsy, she looks for things they all want to do together. Skiing fills the bill. Last year the family traveled to California to ski and visit national parks. "We had such a great time," says Kim animatedly. "It was an educational trip for the kids. Because we all love to ski so much, it brought us together and gave us opportunity to spend true quality time."

The experts speak

> "**S**kiing becomes a safe place to practice risk, enter the unknown, and even fail. And fall. Thank goodness we never stop falling."
>
> —Mermer Blakeslee, master teacher

Mermer Blakeslee, a mentor and coach to many ski teachers, began her skiing career as a racer. She attended Burke Mountain Academy and competed for many years. Leaving racing, she began coaching children at Ski Windham, New York. "I enjoyed teaching," Mermer says. "As I got more involved in it, I became more and more interested in coaching women. There's an energy there that just can't be duplicated in a mixed-gender situation." Now, as a member of the elite National Demonstration Team for the Professional Ski Instructors of America (PSIA), a position she earned through proficiency in skiing and teaching, knowledge, and pure stamina, she continues to make women's education a strong focus.

Mermer founded a program specifically for women called Inside Tracks. "The program is designed to help women turn fear into thrill, connect the mind to the body, and regain a sense of play and exploration. I want women to leave my seminars having learned to relinquish security for adventure and to begin to enjoy the unpredictable."

Mermer believes skiing is a metaphor for life, a way to play with life's issues. "After all, it's only skiing. What an inherently silly thing it is, really. We pay money to go up to come down. Who could be too serious about that? And yet it becomes a safe place to practice risk, enter the unknown, and even fail. And fall. Thank goodness we never stop falling."

Carol Levine is a pioneer in women's ski education. Founder of the Women's College for the Professional Ski Instructors of America, she has provided forums where women ski teachers can learn about gender differences in physical responses, motivation, and technique. These seminars and symposia are dedicated to finding ways to keep more women in the sport. A soft-spoken woman, Carol describes her early years of skiing as social respite. "It was something I could be good at, and as an adolescent I found I needed something physical to measure myself with. I was better

> "**S**kiing is like opening the car window to get wind on your face. When I push off to make a few turns, there's always that feeling of wind on my face."
>
> —Carol Levine, ski educator

than most of my friends, yet there were a few I could strive to catch." Carol took up racing and from there got into coaching racers, then she began coaching the public so as to have a full-time job. "I needed to earn a lift pass to participate in race training, so I signed on to teach skiing part time for the regular ski school. I guess I was good at it," she modestly admits. "It was like a gigantic puzzle. What would work for some people wouldn't work for others, and I got good at figuring it all out. So I stuck with it." Carol is a past member of the Professional Ski Instructors of America's National Demonstration Team. She is currently a training consultant for the ski schools of Vail, Colorado. "Skiing is like opening the car window to get wind on your face. When I push off to make a few turns, there's always that feeling of wind on my face."

Dee Byrne learned to ski with her family in the Northwest, then began teaching so she could stay in the sport. A natural skier, Dee gained recognition from family and friends for her success. When Dee worked with Carol to create the women's event described above, it "piqued my curiosity. I wanted to find out if there really were differences in the way women and men learn to ski. What I found out is that the more you learn about those differences, the more dangerous you become as a teacher. It's very easy to make generalizations that border on prejudice and stop the learning process. I want women to enter the sport with resources to keep them participating." Also a past National Demonstration Team member, Dee currently manages the ski school at Lion's Head in Vail, Colorado.

I have been fortunate to know all of these women, and each one has fueled my own passion for skiing and for sharing it with others. Whether skiing becomes your passion or playtime, hobby or cause, there's room for all of it. As you read the following pages, picture yourself on the mountain, connecting with the snow and making your own turns!

TACKLING "WHAT IF"

Skiing is known as a "risk" sport. Speed and gravity, aerial lifts, extreme snow conditions and weather, and athletes who push the limits contribute to the notoriety. Yet skiing can range from family adventure for kids as young as three to epic adventure on mountains accessible only from aircraft.

Compare skiing to bicycling. Remember learning to ride a two-wheeler? What about riding that two-wheeler to visit a friend? Now imagine a nice long ride on an open road, flat for miles and with no traffic. (That part is truly a dream!) The extreme side of biking includes downhill rides over rough mountain terrain, or the well-honed road rider topping forty miles an hour on a hundred-mile race, slipping a bit on a curved road and taking ten in the pack down with her. It's easy enough to imagine those extremes in biking, yet skiing is the same. The learning skier takes risks, just like someone learning to ride a bike. From there the amount of risk and challenge is your own choice. Yet all

> The amount of risk and challenge is your own choice. Yet all who participate are skiers. The mountain provides a home for even the most timid of explorers.

One of the many forms of transportation at a resort, this old-fashioned trolley is an adventure of its own.

who participate are skiers. The mountain provides a home for even the most timid of explorers. The key is preparation, practice, and enjoying every step of the way.

To conquer quantifiable fears such as riding lifts, losing control, and falling, you must have a good coach and communicate your fears. Once they are in the open, your coach can bring you step by step through any of these hurdles and answer all your questions. Once you've been on the slope, learned to slide, turned, and stopped, you'll understand the mechanics and lose the anxiety that comes from lack of knowledge. From then on it's up to you how much you challenge yourself. You always have control of where and when you ski.

Heights

Mountain peaks as pictured in *National Geographic* are tall and exposed: just the thing to unnerve those who fear heights or open spaces. But skiing doesn't always take place at great altitudes or in vast areas. When learning, you'll be in a protected space at the base of the mountain or on a gentle slope farther up. You'll either walk or take a shuttle or lift to the learning slope.

Falling

Don't kid yourself—you *will* fall down. It's common to tip over from time to time while you're learning to balance and slide. Most of these falls are relatively painless physically and only slightly bruising to the ego. During your lesson you'll be in the care of a professional who will help you minimize your time *in* the snow and maximize your time *on* it. Your instructor will encourage you to manage your pace and your movements to prevent repeated falls and will help you discover the easiest way to return upright. When the occasional tip over does occur, try to relax and let yourself go with it. You'll lose less energy to tension and have more available for getting up. Think of falling as making angels in the snow!

Tera Ingraham plays a "fallen angel" after a fall.

Lifts

There are many ways to get to the top of a mountain. Lifts often worry the uninitiated. Tramways, gondolas, chairlifts, and surface lifts such as poma lifts and handle tows are all inspected and serviced regularly. Resort operators must comply with regulations regarding upkeep and inspections in order to operate them. That said, there is more danger from inexperienced riders when loading and unloading lifts than from mechanical failures. Read all lift area signs and get familiar with the procedures for each new lift you encounter.

Chairlifts are particular sources of anxiety for people afraid of heights. When you're learning, you'll be faced with riding one sooner or later, since most modern ski resorts use the chairlift as the main form of uphill transportation. You'll receive careful instruction on using the lift (see chapter 3), and there are built-in safety features should you have problems getting on or off. If you fear heights, the remedy is to ride with someone (even your instructor) who can direct your attention forward, not down, keep you engaged in positive conversation, and help you focus properly when you get off. If you are extremely fearful, take a private lesson with an instructor well versed in this area (see page 26).

Remember that lifts are relatively easy to ride once you learn the ropes. All it takes is a little practice and knowing that everyone who skis has had to learn to do it; many of them have great stories to tell. "Riding chairlifts was not my idea of a relaxing time!" Judy remembers her first few days on skis, when she struggled every time with loading the chairlift. "It wasn't getting on that worried me. I would just freeze as the lift climbed higher into the air. All I could think of was falling out. But once I got more comfortable with the folks I was riding with, I could hold onto the chair, keep the conversation going, and somehow make it to the top. After a few heart-pounding experiences, the rides got easier and easier."

· ·

"**R**iding chairlifts was not my idea of a relaxing time! . . . All I could think of was falling out. . . . But after a few heart-pounding experiences, the rides got easier and easier."

—Judy, age 30, bank officer

· ·

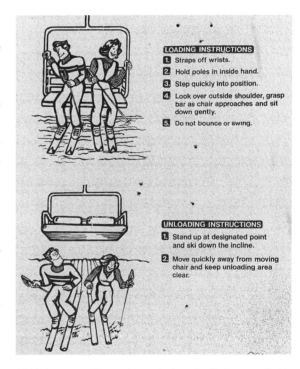

All lifts have posted instructions at the base. Familiarize yourself with all instructions before loading.

● ●

"I've always been active and athletic, but when I ski with certain people I feel inadequate. Maybe it's because they ski more often, they know more good skiers, or they make it look so damned easy!"

—Kim, age 40, nurse practitioner

● ●

Mimi cheers following some particularly exciting turns.

Intangible anxieties

Now for those "other" issues; self-doubt, insecurity, fear of failure, dread of looking "out of place" or not being "one of them." This is the crux of why many women avoid skiing. As a learner, it's easy to feel out of step socially and self-conscious physically.

Here are some stories from women who have wondered if a Caribbean cruise would have been a better choice. When Judy has anxious moments, she relies on talents she uses at work. As a banker, she's used to being in charge. "Suddenly my skis were in an impossible tangle under me," Judy remembers. "I couldn't get them untwisted fast enough, and soon I was in a tangle myself. When I caught my breath I realized I'd fallen in the same place as on the run before. It occurred to me that either I could get mad and go inside or I could figure it out. (But not before a few angry tears had frozen in my goggles!) I went back up the lift, vowing to stay calm and ski through it. When I reached the spot, I looked above me and saw that the ground I'd already covered was just as tricky as my trouble spot. I tried to remember the sensations and images I'd experienced getting there, then I imagined myself skiing right through it. And you know what? I did it!"

Using a magnifying glass on each step you've taken toward your adventure will help you recognize your accomplishments. But beware of picking out only the negatives; you'll find what you look for. When you identify your plusses, then you can use them to continue your quest.

"Trying to keep up with some of my friends is a challenge," admits Kim. "I've always been active and athletic, but when I ski with certain people I feel inadequate. Maybe it's because they ski more often, they know more good skiers, or they make it look so damned easy! Anyway, when I push myself to keep up with them, I feel out of control and ungainly. When this happens I force myself to request a run on an easier slope. That way I can relax for a moment, go a little faster if I want to, and get back in the groove. Then I'm ready for the next challenge."

Kim's experience has reminded her to give herself a break when she needs one. It can be hard to ask for a respite, but chances are that if you need refuge, someone else does too. The break

Right: Group of friends enjoying the snow together. **Below right:** Mimi's not sure of the slope below. She'll need tea and cookies when she reaches the bottom.

time gives the psyche an opportunity to reassess the situation and prepare for the next assault. I firmly believe that hot chocolate breaks were invented to provide warmth not just to the body, but to the spirit as well.

Mermer Blakeslee's seminars often return to this principle. When you're challenged, you spend time in what she calls the "yikes" zone. A person can spend only so much time there without returning to comfort or, as Mermer puts it "tea and cookies." If you learn to recognize your "yikes" zone, it will be easier to stretch your tolerance by knowing when to return to your comfort zone.

Of course, there are other common fears when entering the sport of skiing:

- **What if I'm not in shape?** You don't have to be a fitness junkie to succeed at skiing. No special "body type" is required. You don't have to be skinny or muscular or even particularly well coordinated. Being able to walk pretty much clinches it—and even if you have a disability there are myriad ways to get you on the slopes! Refer to pages 56 to 57 on ways to get yourself ready and maintain your energy level during your first experience.

- **Am I too old for this?** You're never too old! One of my favorite coaching encounters was with a retired couple, Mary and Burt, who had decided to learn together. They were in their late sixties, and they were tired of staying indoors all winter. Mary is tenacious about learning, and she returns for lessons a few times each season. "I think it was easier for me to learn than for Burt. He thought he should be good right away, while I didn't worry about how good I was; I just focused on how good the experience was. That was the secret to success. I forgot my age and used my vast life experiences to help me learn. Now both of us get a tune-up a few times each season."

● **I get cold easily.** Will I be comfortable? Winter temperatures can be daunting until you learn to dress appropriately. Pages 28 to 31 have advice on how to dress for success. If you bundle up well, the cold, brisk air can be rejuvenating.

Remember to congratulate yourself on each new conquest. From reading this book to making contact with a resort, practicing in your living room, packing your ski gear, and making reservations, you've begun the ascent of the mountain. As you start learning, congratulate yourself in the same way. There are a lot of steps, and each step is a journey to be savored and enjoyed.

Chapter 2

INSIDER TIPS FOR A GOOD BEGINNING

Although skiing is thought of as risky, being prepared and knowing what to expect greatly reduces the chance of injury. Skiing is no more dangerous than going for a hike or driving your car on the freeway. As with both these ventures, however, you need some preparation. The least risky way to learn to ski is to take part in an educational program where an experienced professional brings you along step by step so you don't get in over your head. Many learners tackle slopes that are too steep

The least risky way to learn to ski is to take part in an educational program where an experienced professional brings you along step by step so you don't get in over your head.

too soon, often encouraged by well-meaning friends or relatives. Even if they don't get hurt, this negative experience can be hard to overcome on later outings.

Skiing offers a great many options. As we saw from the stories in the first chapter, the applications are as varied as the people who ski. Don't let that overwhelm you—getting started is essentially the same for everyone. The best decision you can make is to take lessons from an expert, perhaps in a ski program that will take you from learner to independent explorer. Ideal learning sessions provide information on equipment and clothing, are well paced, and provide follow-up experiences.

The choices at most resorts include everything from one two-hour lesson to a three-step program to a full-blown ski week. All these options can be tailored with group sessions or private coaching. The best one for you depends on your learning style, your social preferences or needs, and of course how close you live to the mountains.

> "I knew that I needed to be given a logical and methodical series of steps to be comfortable. When I got on the slope, I asked lots of questions so I could create those steps."
>
> —Judy, age 30, bank officer

LEARNING STYLE

Take a moment to examine your learning style and determine your comfort levels. When was the last time you learned a new skill? If you can recall that experience, the parts you enjoyed and the parts you found uncomfortable, you'll gain valuable insight into what avenue will produce the most success and yield the most fun.

When Judy learned to ski, she remembered learning a new computer system at work. "I'm pretty step-by-step as a rule. I knew that I needed to be given a logical and methodical series of steps to be comfortable. When I got on the slope, I asked lots of questions so I could create those steps." Reflecting on her experience helped Judy participate more fully and learn faster.

- Do you explore new things easily, or do you like step-by-step direction? If you like personal feedback every step of the way or are particularly fearful or cautious, you'll be more comfortable with individual instruction.

- If you're adventurous by nature or if you like to get a little direction and then spend time figuring things out for yourself, you'll be more likely to enjoy a group situation. If you prefer to learn in the company of others or like cooperative learning, group programs are your style.

Social considerations

Probably the most important ingredient is who will be traveling to the mountains with you. Skiing is an individual sport that is enhanced by the company of others. Whether you'll be skiing with family, joining friends, or looking for new horizons is a key factor in determining the best learning situation.

- If you'll be learning with your family, ask for a program that includes family instruction. Usually children and adults are separated to make communication and pacing easier, yet more and more resorts are providing for families that want to learn together. Ask specifically for teachers who have experience with all the age groups in your family, and be sure to plan for at least a half-day program (four hours) with breaks to allow for practice and warm-ups.

- If you're joining friends at the resort, try to take charge of your own learning right from the start. Call the resort directly and get information on learning programs yourself. This way you can ask the questions you need to prepare yourself and won't have to rely on others for this important first step. Remember, if your friends already know how to ski, they may think they know the resort well (and perhaps they do), but they probably are not familiar with the services learners need. They may not even know which area is best for new skiers.

- Call ahead to be sure you know about program options, and prepare for an exciting new way to see the outdoors in winter. Special programs are springing up around the country that offer lessons for women only. This is often a more comfortable and supportive way to learn, not to mention that lasting friendships may be created through the shared experience. (See pages 83–84.)

Practical considerations

- How close are you to the mountains? Are you looking for the big resort vacation or just a day's getaway? Or do you live near a ski area that offers several evening sessions spread over four to six weeks?

- How fit are you? Enjoying skiing doesn't require a cardiovascular superwoman, but learning a new outdoor sport will require exertion and bring new muscles into play. Can you handle an all-inclusive two-hour program, or would you be better with a half- or full-day lesson that is slower paced and less intense? (See pages 55–58 for more details on fitness.)

- Call ahead, and speak directly to a program administrator. There are many departments at a ski resort, and the reservationists may not have all the answers you need. Find out what your options are, when the programs are offered, and whether you need reservations, and ask for written program descriptions and maps of the area. (See pages 36–38.)

DOES YOUR COACH HAVE THE "RIGHT STUFF"?

The most crucial ingredient of your learning experience is your coach. In group lessons you may not know ahead of time who your teacher will be or what his or her credentials are. But if you're taking a private session you can request specific traits to make your comfort and success more

LESSON COSTS

For group lessons, expect to spend $30 to $50, depending on the duration of the lesson. The cost decreases per day as you purchase more days.

For private lessons, you'll pay $65 to $85 an hour. The hourly cost decreases as you add time. Five hours runs from $300 to $900. You can also bring a friend for a small add-on fee.

• •

"Finding a good coach is one of the most important ingredients for success. . . . He or she can provide you with much more than a ski lesson."

—Dee Byrne, ski school manager

• •

likely. "Finding a good coach is one of the most important ingredients for success," states Dee Byrne. "After all, of all the staff members at a resort, you'll spend the most time in the company of your coach. He or she can provide you with much more than a ski lesson." Here are some important questions to ask when connecting with a professional:

- How long has the pro been teaching, both in general and at the specific resort?

- What special credentials does the pro have? (Skill with children, women, or teens? Foreign languages? Degrees in communication or education?)

- Is the pro certified with either a resort-specific program or the Professional Ski Instructors of America? At what level of certification?

- What is the pro's track record in guest service and return business?

- What kind of training program does the resort have? Has your pro been trained step by step? Smaller resorts often rely solely on a pro's experience. If so, be sure to ask for someone who's been working there at least a couple of seasons. If you can't get this in group lessons, consider a private coach or a women's group.

Other requests to consider when scheduling a specific professional are

- Does the pro have an open schedule to allow you to repeat the lesson?

- Would you be more comfortable with a man or a woman?

- Is there a pro who has been trained specifically for the situation (first-time skiers, women, families)?

After your lesson, it's time to evaluate whether your coach was right for you. Jan wryly recalls, "I thought I was slow or something. My teacher never spoke directly to me, and I always felt a beat behind. It never occurred to me that it might be the coach and not me!" Do a little reflection following your lesson. Do you feel good about the experience? Would you like to repeat it? Do you think you'll be able to ski better each time you work with that coach? Were you inspired by the relationship, or do you have a slightly negative feeling about yourself and skiing in general? Do you feel overwhelmed? If the negative emotions are the ones you've identified, try a different coach. Resist the urge to assume it's "just me." Most resorts will work with you to find a good match if you ask the right questions. The object is to keep you in the sport, not drain your pocketbook.

Learning from your "best friend"

Many women try to learn from friends or lovers. This is usually a big mistake. First of all, teaching anything is a talent and a profession. Knowing how to ski does not make a person capable of teaching someone else. This problem is compounded when a relationship is at stake. "He assumed that since I was athletic I would pick it right up," Mary (not her real name), anxiously explained, "so he took me right up the lift, and I spent nearly the whole day struggling my way down. It was a long time before I could enjoy myself skiing after that. It put a real strain on my relationship with him." And Mary is not the exception. Many women let their boyfriends or husbands take charge simply because they know how to ski. Sadly, many amateurs don't take the time to find out what will make a learner most comfortable. Usually they learned so long ago that they've forgotten what it's like. Even worse, they expect their learning friend to join them on more advanced slopes right away. That just isn't reasonable, and the expectation often causes discord. Better to plan separate experiences until you're proficient on learning slopes and understand the layout of a resort well enough to let your partner know where you'll be comfortable skiing.

Of course there are always exceptions, and Judy is one of these. Her husband is a certified ski teacher, and he understood enough about the needs of learning skiers—and about his wife— to be an effective teacher. Judy was very fearful at the beginning, yet he recognized that she was a step-by-step learner and cared about detail. He coached her to work on specific movements and gave her enough specifics that she didn't have time to worry about being afraid. It was the perfect mix for her. "He'd give me a specific thing to work on and tell me where to practice, and I'd spend hours on my own perfecting the movements while he was teaching others. Then we'd get back together and I'd show him what I'd done. It kept me busy while he was working, and it was exciting to share what I had accomplished. He was always careful to tell me just how far I'd progressed and to recognize my accomplishment, which is what I'm in it for. My motivation is to keep getting better, and he knows that."

• •

"**F**rom that point I began to participate in my own learning. It was give and take, and I worked just as hard as she did."

—Kim, age 40, nurse practitioner

• •

BEING A GOOD LEARNER

A lot of attention is given to making sure the teacher is right for you, but any ideal learning situation reflects what the Professional Ski Instructors of America call "the learning partnership." This means learners must be empowered to take responsibility for their own accomplishments. While this is in part the teacher's job, it's also yours.

Kim remembers a private lesson where she felt she'd nearly missed the boat. "When the teacher asked what I wanted to work on, I just deferred to her. I thought she should know what I needed more than I did. Partway through the lesson it became clear to me that I wanted to get off the same old slopes I'd been skiing all morning, and that if I didn't tell her soon, it might not happen! I spoke up, and from that point I began to participate in my own learning. It was give and take, and I worked just as hard as she did."

What can you do to assume your part of this responsibility? Let your coach know your goals. Give all your attention to the learning at hand, or at least as much as you can. If you have any problems either physically or mentally, describe them for your teacher. Make sure you do your part to keep communication open. Making your needs clear opens a dialogue that will bring more success. Remember, a teacher who doesn't know you are cold, tired, or anxious might be able to figure it out, but time will be wasted on guessing rather than spent teaching you.

WHAT TO WEAR

Don't underestimate the importance of proper clothing for your first outing on snow. Getting cold or wet can shorten the time you feel like putting in. It's relatively simple to dress well for your first day of skiing, and chances are you own most or all of the necessary items. The only thing you'll need to do is plan. (See chapter 7.)

Layering is the key to coping with frigid alpine temperatures. The first layer should be long underwear of man-made materials such as polypropylene. Cotton may feel great, but it doesn't retain warmth when wet and doesn't wick moisture away from the skin.

A second layer such as a turtleneck will keep additional heat in, especially in a particularly cool or damp climate.

Long underwear should be close-fitting yet comfortable, and made of material that wicks moisture away from the skin.

• •

It's relatively simple to dress well for your first day of skiing, and chances are you own most or all of the necessary items.

• •

These also come in synthetics. Next add a wool sweater or wind-stopping fleece. A pair of insulated, waterproof pants that fit over the tops of your boots completes the layers below, and an insulated, water-resistant, and windproof parka or jacket completes the top.

If you're in a climate where it might rain, don't fret—plenty of companies make great rain gear for skiing. Don't wear a slicker, though, since the slippery surface can be downright dangerous if you fall. Dee Byrne remembers skiing with her mom in the rain. Noticing too late that her mother wore a slicker, she saw her fall and slide a frightening distance. Yet snow conditions in the rain can be easy to learn on, and skiing then can be quite pleasant once you get used to the idea.

Accessories are just as important as the basic layers. The body steals heat and circulation from the extremities to keep the core warm, so plan to wear one pair of wool or synthetic athletic socks. These should be smooth (no ribbing) and long enough to cover your calves. Invest in a good pair of socks, and if your feet tend to get cold, get a couple of pairs so you can change them at midday (even if you think your feet don't sweat, they'll become moist and may get chilled). "There's almost nothing harder to convince people of than wearing only one pair of socks. I spend hours on my hands and knees helping people get into their boots. Half of those hours are spent explaining that two pair of socks will rub and bunch and cause pain," states Maura, a ski teacher from California.

Gloves or mittens should be waterproof or water resistant and insulated and should let you move easily. You won't want to be removing them outside any more than necessary. If you're prone to cold extremities, you can purchase handwarmer packets that go inside your gloves or mittens. These are wonderful on very cold days. "I probably ski at least five or six days more each year now that I can use my handwarmers," Maura says. Mittens are usually warmer, but gloves offer more freedom of movement. It's a personal choice.

Top: There are many stylish options for pants and parkas. Just be sure what you choose is water-resistant and comfortable. **Above:** Just because it's raining doesn't mean you have to get wet. There are many ways to be stylish and dry at the same time. Sometimes the best snow surfaces develop during a rainfall.

Double layers of socks can bunch up and cause pain. Wear only one pair of socks in boots that fit correctly.

Headgear is extremely important because you can lose up to 90 percent of your body heat through your head. Covering it with a wool or fleece hat will keep you more comfortable in cold temperatures. Resist worrying about a bad hair day; "hat head" is a small price to pay for staying warm. It's hard to emphasize this point enough, but even when it's sunny and nice at the bottom of a mountain, the top can have a whole different weather pattern. At the very least, carry the hat with you. You'll be more comfortable and ski longer if you do.

Another headgear option is a helmet. Many skiers are now wearing helmets for the same reasons bicyclists do. Other skiers can't always control their actions, and a helmet offers some protection. The same logic applies as with a seat belt: you don't need one if you aren't in an accident, but you do if you are. Again, it's a personal choice.

For those really cold days, add a fleece neck gaiter (scarves are a no-no because they can get caught in the lift mechanism). They can be found at most ski shops. A neoprene face mask will help prevent frostbite. Also look for fleece vests that can be added over or under other layers. The more layers, the more air is trapped between them to serve as insulation. Also, thin layers promote mobility, whereas thick, bulky clothing can make movement difficult.

There are really warm days in the mountains. If you're lucky enough to hit a sunny, warm day, remember that the higher you go, the colder it can be. Even if you can wear a T-shirt and shorts in the village, the resort may be as much as twenty degrees colder. Be prepared and wear layers that can be shed. You may be more comfortable in a headband instead of a hat. But don't take off the gloves! The metal edges on your skis, when properly tuned, are

Above left: There is a wide variety of options for gloves and mittens. Pick the ones that work for you. **Left:** On warm days, a headband provides a cooler alternative to a hat.

extremely sharp. Given the right (that is, wrong) circumstances, the edge can slice through unprotected skin like a knife. You can find lightweight gloves that will protect your hands. My son, at age ten, was skiing with friends on a warm spring day and took off his gloves. He happened to fall, and his buddy skied over his hand and nearly severed all the ligaments. If he'd been wearing gloves it wouldn't have been an issue.

Finally, don't forget the sunscreen! The sun's rays are magnified by the snow surface, and sunburn can ruin a brilliant vacation. (See pages 54–55 on sunscreen and on sunglasses and goggles.)

Val Emore shows off her stylish new helmet.

RENTING GEAR

Chances are your first time on skis will be with rented gear. Most programs will package gear rental with lessons, and this is usually the best option. Trying to save money by borrowing equipment from a friend usually just isn't safe or smart. First, you don't know how well that equipment has been cared for or if it has been properly maintained for safety. Second, it's not designed specifically for you. Expect to spend anywhere from $20 to $50 a day. Many learning programs include the cost of your rentals. To have the best learning experience, you need boots that fit well, bindings that function properly, and skis designed for a learner. If, as in Judy's case, your friend is a ski teacher and understands these things, it may be worth the risk. But be aware that most major resorts now cater to learners and offer rental equipment that is up to date and maintained for safety and performance. (See pages 98–104 for advice on buying your own gear.)

If your first trip will be to a small resort, it's worth asking how recently their rental equipment was purchased and how often it's serviced during the season. If the rental fleet hasn't been replaced in the past three seasons, then the equipment may be out of date and overused. In this case call around to local sports shops and get a referral to a good rental shop. Many urban ski shops rent equipment so that they can get your business should you decide to buy later, and they'll be motivated to take good care of you. Ski technology is advancing rapidly, and equipment changes a great deal from year to year. Be sure you learn on the best there is.

Remember, the equipment is a big factor in your performance. If you're uncomfortable or don't do well at first, be sure to explore equipment options. Women especially tend to blame themselves before checking for external obstacles to their success.

Renting ski boots

Many types of ski boots are currently in use. There are three basic designs you may encounter.

The first type is a basic overlap shell that you put on by spreading the buckles and sliding your foot in from the top. This is the commonest and most functional type of boot. Although it

overlap-entry boot   midentry boot   rear-entry boot

Three options of boot design.

may be the most difficult to get a foot into, it's the best for performance because it hugs your foot closely and transmits movement to the skis more readily. This means more control, especially while learning.

The second type, a midentry boot, is hinged so it can be entered from the center. Many rental programs use this type for its ease of entry and comfort, yet performance is not quite as accurate as with the overlap style.

The third type, a rear-entry boot, has a hinge that pulls the rear of the boot away. This boot was extremely popular a few years back for its ease of entry, comfort, and warmth, but most programs are now moving away from it, since this design tends to affect balance adversely. However, some programs keep these boots on hand for special fit challenges.

Whatever type of boots you use, it's crucial that they fit well. Wear one pair of thin polypropylene socks without ribbing that reach to your knees. Socks are a key element in boot fit, warmth, and comfort. Cotton socks retain moisture, ribbed socks tend to rub the shins, and thick socks will blunt sensations between the foot and the snow. Ski boots will not fit like a well-worn sneaker, or even a new hiking boot. They'll feel a lot more snug, yet there should be no painful spots. Common complaint areas are around the ankles, the top of the foot, the toes, and the shins. If you feel any pain, let the person fitting your boots know so that adjustments can be made. Finally, don't expect to be able to rent women's boots: resorts don't necessarily carry both men's (unisex) and women's boots in their rental shops. (For information on buying your own boots, see pages 98–100.)

Bindings

Bindings are critical to your safety while skiing. They're designed to keep your feet attached to the skis except when they need to release, as in a fall. This is a complex proposition, but manufacturers have handled it well. Bindings designed in the past four or five years do this essential job very well. Reputable rental programs regularly test each binding on each ski, but you must have them adjusted properly and understand how they work.

Typical rental boots.

"TRADITIONAL" AND "SHAPED" SKIS

• •

All skis have *sidecut*, defined by the Professional Ski Instructors of America as "the characteristic of skis, when lying flat on the snow and viewed from above, to display greater width at the tips and tails than at the middle." The new technology gives "shaped" skis a more pronounced sidecut than traditional skis. Newer, shaped skis are designed to turn in a specific radius. Generally speaking, the tighter the turn radius, the easier it is to turn the ski.

A salesperson shows the distinct differences in ski shapes.

At the rental shop, you'll fill out a release form that lists your height, weight, and skiing ability. It's important to provide this information accurately, since the bindings' performance relies on it.

Once the technician has the necessary information, the binding is fitted to the size of your boot and adjusted according to your weight and ability. Finally, you'll be shown how to enter and exit the binding.

Skis

In choosing skis to learn on it's important to consider length, degree of stiffness both along the length of the ski and across its width, and shape. For your first ski lessons you'll use a shorter ski than you'll eventually be using. Some learning programs are trying extremely short skis at first and moving students up to longer lengths as they progress. This used to be called the "graduated length

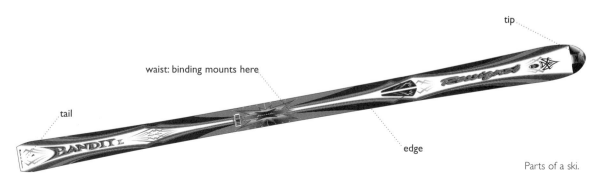

tip

waist: binding mounts here

tail

edge

Parts of a ski.

Left: GLM has enjoyed a resurgence of late. With the advent of shaped skis, the "graduated length method" has enjoyed renewed success for learners. Below left: Be sure to use pole straps properly to avoid injuring your thumb.

method" or GLM. Many programs still use the acronym, but it now stands for "graduated learning method," "guaranteed learning method," or another variation. The basic concept is still the same.

In any case, learn on a ski that is no taller than you are; shorter is probably better. The main objective of your first outing will be to learn basic movements and how to move your body to control the ski. You'll be on relatively gentle slopes, and your skis should allow you to move freely and easily. Many shops are now renting shaped skis (see page 33). (For information on buying your own skis, see pages 100–102.)

Poles

Ski poles are used for balance, to help you get up from a fall, to release your bindings, and to push you across the flats when you run out of hill. You may practice movements without them in your first lessons, but poles are definitely part of skiing, so you should get some and be sure they're the right size.

Poles are usually the last consideration for a rental shop and are often the items most used and abused. Be sure that yours have shafts free of bends and angles and that they swing easily. (Some poles are designed with curves, but these are meant for racing. There are also "corrective angle" poles.) The grip (where you hold the pole) should be sized appropriately for your hand, and the straps should be roomy enough so you can slide your hand through with a glove or mitten on, yet not so long that they're awkward. When sizing poles in the shop, turn the pole over, hold it beneath the basket, and check that your elbow forms a ninety-degree angle. Poles that are too long get in the way; those that are too short interfere with your balance.

To hold poles properly, slide your hand up through the strap from the bottom and grasp pole and strap together. This gives you greater control of the pole. A common injury, "skier's thumb," occurs when a skier tries to break a fall with an outstretched hand that is holding a ski pole. This injury requires rehabilitation and often surgery, yet many skiers ignore it and end up with a permanently weakened thumb.

grip

strap

shaft

basket

tip

Parts of a pole.

Holding the pole and strap correctly helps you avoid this injury. If your poles have no straps, be sure you can grasp the plastic grips completely and swing the pole easily. Although they're not the best, strapless grips will be fine on your first trip. (See pages 102–3 for purchasing recommendations.)

Be sure it's the best

As a new skier, you'll probably be renting your equipment for the first two or three times. Here's a checklist of items that will affect the performance of the skis. If the skis are unacceptable on one or more of these points, ask for a different pair or take your business elsewhere.

1. Be sure your boot fits in the bindings. Sometimes one binding is overlooked or set for the wrong size boot. Double-check before you leave the shop.

2. Your DIN (Deutsche industrie normen), the setting that determines the point when the bindings release, will be determined by a chart based on your skiing ability, weight, height, and age. A small window on the binding shows the number. The rental technician should show this to you and explain it. If not, ask. You'll need to sign a form certifying that the shop technician set your DIN, that you looked at it, and that it was correct when you left the shop. Be sure to check both skis.

3. Run your fingers along the edges of the skis. Be careful, since they could be sharp enough to cut you. You can protect your fingers with a small piece of tissue. If you can feel large irregularities or gouges in the edges, or if the tissue gets caught, request that the edges be checked or ask for a different pair. Gouges or irregularities can detract considerably from the performance of the skis, especially in firm snow conditions.

4. Place the skis base to base and rub them together sideways. If there's a loud clicking noise or if you can feel the edges catching each other significantly, the edges may be railed (raised above the base), which can make the ski more difficult to turn. Again, ask for a different pair.

5. Look at the bottoms of the skis. Small nicks and scrapes in the base material shouldn't cause much problem, but if there are large holes, exposing the insides, ask for another set. Also, check to be sure the bases have been waxed recently. If they look grayish or dry, get them replaced.

If you'll be using the same equipment for more than a couple of days, you may want to have the edges checked if you find any new gouges or other changes at the end of the day. Many people who own their skis get the edges retuned every five to ten times they go skiing, more often if there's a problem. If you're not sure about the condition of your skis, ask your teacher or bring them to the repair shop to be checked.

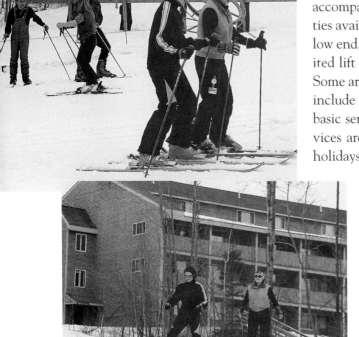

CHOOSING THE RIGHT RESORT

Considerations such as distance from home, who will accompany you, the size of the resort, and the amenities available will help you choose where to go. At the low end, expect to pay as little as $50 for a lesson, limited lift ticket, and equipment at the smallest resorts. Some areas with their own lodging have packages that include an overnight stay, starting around $75 for basic services. In general, these prices increase as services are added, as the resort size goes up, or during holidays or weekends. You should explore a resort for learners, but learning is only part of the equation. It's important to decide what kind of total experience you're looking for.

Smaller resorts

At small resorts there's usually less hustle and bustle, you get more personal attention, and it's easier to find your way around. Smaller resorts often cater to novices, and the slopes are less crowded and more conducive to learning. Many offer special multi-day learning packages, even in the evenings so you can attend after work. But these local resorts can get crowded and busy if they're close to cities, and they may not provide many amenities.

Top: Learning is part of the resort experience. **Above:** Lodging is often so close to the slopes that you can ski right to your door—no cars necessary!

One of my favorite experiences was when I went to a very small resort to train a group of ski teachers. I brought my two children, then six and seven. It turned out to be one of my favorite days of skiing, and one they remember too, because they were able to explore the trails on their own.

The plan was that they would stay with my group on the hill, but they soon tired of this and became disruptive. While waiting to load the lift, they asked me loudly if they could ski on their own. The burly lift attendant asked if he could help by keeping an eye on them, as did a nearby patroller. I was able to continue my work, while my children felt like grown-ups. It was wonderful knowing they would be looked after and would also be having a great day. That personal touch is often possible only at local resorts.

Learning is only part of the equation. It's important to decide what kind of total experience you're looking for.

Medium-sized resorts

Resorts of a moderate size can offer the best of both worlds. Depending on their location, they can provide less crowded slopes and more variety. These resorts often have lodging on or near the mountain, with more resort-based activities.

The big ones

Larger resorts usually offer more—but more is not always better, unless, of course, you understand what you need and are ready to take advantage of all the amenities. Larger resorts also have a range of pricing that is an advantage over fixed rates of smaller places.

Once you've decided to visit a particular region of the country to learn, it's always a good idea to call and ask specific questions about resorts and their programs. This will help you to choose which one is right for you and tell you what to expect and how to prepare for your adventure. The following list of questions will get you enough information to plan well.

1.   What programs do you offer for someone who's never skied before?

2.   What ages do these programs include?

3.   How much do they cost?

4.   Does the price include equipment, lift access, or both?

5.   Can I keep my equipment for the whole day or just while I'm in the lesson?

6.   Is there limited trail access or full mountain access?

7.   How long is the instructional program?

8.   When is the program offered? Do I need a reservation?

9.   If I make a reservation, do I prepay? What if I need to cancel?

10. Are there package deals that offer multiple experiences or include lodging?

11. If I arrive the day before, can I reserve my equipment then?

12. Are there any promotions where I can get a special deal?

13. If equipment isn't included, where should I rent it? How much will it cost?

14. If equipment is included, what brand is offered and how old is it? How often is it maintained? (This will let you know whether to rent equipment elsewhere and bring it with you.)

15. On what basis are groups formed? Can I choose to learn with other women?

16.   How is the staff for the learning program trained? Do they have any special credentials, or can I request someone who does?

17.   Can you send me a written description of the program and the resort?

18.   Can you send a resort map with program and check-in locations marked?

19.   How much time should I allow to reach the learning center when I arrive at the resort?

20.   Is there parking nearby, or should I allow extra time to ride a shuttle or find other transportation?

21.   Is there storage space near the ski school? Should I bring change for lockers and such?

22.   Are meals and snacks available, or should I bring my own?

Don't assume the program will be canceled because of what you may perceive as inclement weather. Remember, skiing is a winter sport, and weather usually affects only what clothing is appropriate. Extreme weather is just part of the adventure! High winds, blizzards, avalanches, or torrential rains may require a change in plans, however. Whether you have a reservation or not, call the resort for information and options.

WHEN YOU ARRIVE FOR THE DAY

Be sure to leave plenty of time to get your ducks in a row after you arrive at the resort. Just driving into the parking lot in time does not guarantee you are home free. You've just begun. Many resorts have multiple base areas, and learning centers may or may not be accessible from all of them. Be sure the lot you park in is where you need to be. If you're not sure, there are usually parking attendants who can answer your questions. If you have a lot of gear (or if you brought your family or friends, or lunch, or whatever), there are often drop-off zones where you can leave your car for a few minutes while you unload. But be sure to plan how you'll rendezvous with your companions. In some cases you'll need to ride a shuttle to the base area after parking. Be sure you get clear descriptions of where you'll be let off when you return and how late the shuttles run at the end of the day. The last thing you want is a long, cold walk after an exhilarating day on the slopes.

When you leave your car, be sure you can lock up any gear you bring with you. A resort is like a little community, and there are always a few unsavory types watching for their chance. Be sure you're not the next victim: stow your gear in lockers and leave all unneeded items locked in your car. If you bring equipment, be sure you have a lock for it (they're usually available in resort shops) or put it in a locking rack. Another option is a checkroom where you pay a small fee and have unlimited access to your equipment throughout the day.

Above: Checking equipment provides peace of mind. **Right:** Time your arrival so you meet a relaxing scene such as this one. Long lines at prime times make for frazzled nerves.

Before you separate from friends or family, be sure to look around and set a time to meet. Make an alternative plan too. Expect the unexpected. In unfamiliar surroundings and with a new sport, it's difficult to tell how long things will take. Besides, you might just be having too much fun to be on time for a rendezvous!

WHEN YOU ARRIVE FOR AN OVERNIGHT STAY

Multiple-day options often give you the most bang for your buck. Be sure to ask about discounts and about what can be packaged together, such as lifts, lodging, rentals, and lessons.

When you're staying longer than one day, arriving the day before you begin your adventure will give you time to acclimate to the resort and be fresh. It also allows you more space (your room) to stow gear and a quiet place to crash when needed. Check to see if there are special evening orientation programs. Many larger resorts use these to answer questions. Be sure you know all the resources the resort has to offer.

A multiday experience will also let you pace your learning so you don't feel rushed and give you ample time to practice during the day and to enjoy the resort lifestyle at night. Après-ski amusements include clubs with bands, restaurants, shopping, health clubs and spas, and such. When you check in you'll be given a guide to these activities. If it's not offered, be sure to ask.

When you check in at the resort, ask specifically about checking in to your learning program. You may need to plan extra time to catch a shuttle or bus. You may also need to call to confirm your attendance. You may even be able to streamline your check-in procedures before arriving at the learning center. This is especially important to explore on vacation weeks or busy weekends.

Chapter 3

WHAT TO EXPECT FROM YOUR FIRST SKI ADVENTURE

N ow that you're prepared to make travel arrangements and assemble the gear for your adventure, it's time to prepare your mind and body to learn the basics of the sport so you'll get the most from your excursion.

SKIING IN YOUR LIVING ROOM

> "I couldn't believe it: I never thought I'd feel so comfortable! . . . I can't wait for tomorrow!"
>
> —Beverly, age 45, mother of three teenagers

Let's take a moment to look at what skiing truly is. In chapter 1 skiing was described as a creative dance, an intimate connection between body, mind, and spirit. When you're mastering the movements, however, the mind comes to the fore and helps the body learn. Since you're reading this book, chances are you're the type of learner who wants a preview—a way to engage the brain first and get an overview. In terms of simple physics, in skiing we're controlling descent down a mountain face by using a tactic that lets us defy gravity—turning away from its inevitable force. To ski well, therefore, you must learn to turn efficiently and effectively in any conditions of snow, slope, or speed.

The path of gravity is called the *fall line* because it's the route an object would follow in rolling or sliding freely downhill. If you look at the basic diagram of the slope, you'll see how we

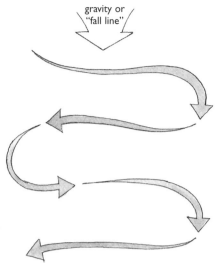

gravity or "fall line"

Left: Skier's path to maintain speed down a slope. **Below:** The author playing with gravity.

can control the force of gravity by turning out of its pull and *across* the slope, crossing and recrossing the fall line. To stop or slow down, you simply turn uphill. Once you've learned to do this, you'll learn to dance with gravity's pull so your turns are in graceful cooperation with the mountain.

In your very first lessons, focus on feeling gravity pulling you toward a turn. As you can see in the diagram, you have to go with gravity to get away from it again. Once you know this logically, you can stay confident and focused when your body takes over in the pure reaction to sliding.

Basic movements

There are some very basic movements that you can practice at home on the living room rug to help prepare you for your first adventure on skis. These movements will repeat themselves at all levels of skiing and in all conditions of snow and slope. Although there are endless variations in how these movements are applied, just experiencing the sensations they create in stocking feet can give you a big head start both physically and mentally. Practice them a few times in front of a mirror before you get to the slopes, and you'll start with confidence and advance more quickly.

First, assume a basic athletic stance. This is the "ready" stance used in tennis, baseball, basketball, and many other sports. Facing a mirror, stand with your feet hip width apart, toes pointed straight forward, hips, knees, and ankles slightly flexed. You should feel that you can move quickly in any direction from this position. Your weight should feel centered, not forward over the toes or back over the heels. When you're skiing you'll be sliding forward, yet you'll still be in this basic stance.

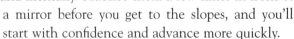

The living room is a great place to practice basic balance.

Turning

From this position, move your toes slightly inward. This position is called a *wedge* because when you have skis and boots on your skis will form a wedge shape. Now move your toes back. Try to create a pivot point at the middle of your feet. Move one foot at a time, then both feet. Notice that the movement begins at your hip socket, not at your knee or foot. This is the basic movement you'll use to turn your skis.

When you're actually skiing, however, your ski boots and skis tend to distract you from the sensations you can feel in stocking feet. Remember these sensations and search for them when you venture outside. Try to imagine how it will feel when you are sliding on the surface of the snow.

Tipping

Return to the basic stance. Now roll both knees slowly to the right, then to the left. You should feel the edges of the soles of your feet. If this is difficult, try flexing your ankles either more or less. Be sure your body is lined up correctly. Hold your arms out to the sides to help you balance, and focus on what you feel. This will introduce you to the movements needed to tip your skis on their edges.

Bending

Now stand with your weight centered between both feet. Move slowly so that all your weight is on your left foot, then slowly move through center to the right. Try to stay balanced as you move. Again, imagine yourself sliding on skis. Perform this simple movement low to the floor, with hips, knees, and ankles extremely flexed, then do it in a very tall stance. This exercise will help you learn to move from one foot to the other or one ski to the other to manage pressures between the ski and the snow.

Top left: The best place to practice the wedge is inside, where it's warm! **Above:** Tipping the feet is best learned without ski boots on. Once you master the movement this way, you'll find it easier on snow. **Left:** As you put more weight on one foot or the other, the weighted ski will bend more, determining the arc of your turn.

Focus on what it takes to turn your feet, roll your feet onto their sides, and shift your weight from one foot to the other and on how it feels. Your ski teacher will help you combine these

As skiing matures as a sport . . . learning is recognized as a central component in its continuation, so resorts are spending more time and money to create a welcoming atmosphere and an optimal environment for learners.

movements to create turns later on. For now, just store up the sensations you feel here on the living room rug.

YOUR FIRST TRIP TO THE SLOPES

Your first hour on skis will be exciting and challenging—exciting because you'll embark on a new way to explore the outdoors, challenging because you'll be bombarded with new sensations. You'll learn to glide, slide, climb, get up from a fall, and begin to turn, all in that first hour.

Your first assignment will be to get your gear and meet your instructor at a designated place. Many resorts are now asking first timers to meet their teachers inside in a special area designed for you to get acquainted. Your instructor will check your gear, show you how to operate your bindings, be sure you have the right clothing for the day's weather, and then lead you to the learning slope.

You'll begin on a slope designed for lessons—sometimes lovingly referred to as the bunny hill. As skiing matures as a sport, however, learning is recognized as a central component in its continuation, so resorts are spending more time and money to create a welcoming atmosphere and an optimal environment for learners. Your learning area will likely be near the program headquarters or ski lodge. It will have a very flat area where you can practice basic movements, including stationary maneuvers like the ones you did in your living room. If your program uses traditional skis or longer shaped skis, you may practice first wearing just the boots or even using one ski at a time. If you begin with very short skis, you may practice basics with both skis right away.

CARRYING YOUR SKIS

Manage your skis by placing them base to base, allowing the ski brakes to interlock at the *waist,* or middle, of the ski. Pick up your skis by standing them on their tails, turning your back to them, and guiding them onto your shoulder. This leaves your other hand free to manage your poles. Carry the skis' weight on your shoulder and balance them with your hand. Reverse this process when putting them down. When other skiers are nearby, be sure to hold skis upright. Wear gloves whenever you handle your skis to keep your fingers warm and prevent your palms from being pinched.

Carrying skis is more comfortable if you wear gloves or mittens, which also protect your hands from the sharp edges of the skis.

Balancing while sliding on skis is a new sensation for most people.

GETTING FRIENDLY WITH YOUR SKIS

Skis can go on either foot; there's no right or left. The front of the ski is called the *tip*, and the back is called the *tail*. Before putting your skis on, be sure you have the pair that's adjusted to your boots. Next, take a look at the binding position—the heel piece can be open or closed. If the binding is in its closed position, press the tab down to release it. Place the toe of the boot in the toe piece of the binding and step down firmly with your heel.

The goal for the first hour is to practice basic movements and get you sliding freely. You'll learn the components of gliding, turning, and control. Balancing while sliding on skis is a new sensation for most people, yet if you've ever done ice skating or in-line skating you have a reference.

You probably won't get on a lift right away. You'll need to be comfortable sliding and turning before you ride a chairlift. First you'll practice stationary movements as you did in your living room, then you'll begin to combine these movements with sliding. The first sliding and gliding will be done in a flat area so you can gain confidence. You'll practice sliding, gliding, stepping, and skating movements that will get you comfortable maneuvering your skis and prepare you for slopes with more pitch.

Top: Be sure the bottom of your boot is free of snow before stepping into the binding.
Above: Learning to maneuver on your skis can be a challenge until you learn how to work with gravity.

THE PRACTICE CLIMB

Two exercises that will help you learn to maneuver your skis are sidestepping and "the bull-fighter." First you'll practice stepping up and down a slight incline with your skis parallel to each other and perpendicular to the fall line, like going up and down stairs sideways. In sidestepping you must tip each ski onto its edge by tilting your lower legs to push your knees uphill, and you learn control by feeling the edges grip the snow and seeing how much you slip as you move one ski and bring the other up (or down) to it.

Next you'll practice the *bullfighter* turn. Once you've sidestepped up the slope, turn your body toward the downhill side of your skis and plant both poles below you on the slope, reaching out and down as far as possible and straightening your arms to brace yourself. Then, taking small steps to bring first your ski tips together and then the tails, gradually step around until you're facing your poles and looking downhill. When you're ready, lift your poles and glide down the slope. Be sure you're in a spot where you'll come to a natural stop. Your teacher will pick the right place to practice this.

Left: Practice in boots before you even put your skis on. **Below:** The bullfighter turn will help you with your balance before you glide down the slope. **Bottom:** Your first glides should be in a controlled environment where your skis come to a natural stop.

THE WEDGE

One tool for learning to turn—called the *wedge*—works like training wheels on a bike. When you're comfortable gliding and turning, you'll progress to keeping your skis parallel. To make a wedge, point your ski tips toward each other but leave space between the tips. As you turn, both tips point in the direction of travel, and the ski to the outside of the turn carries most of the load. Glide across the slope in the wedge. Notice you must twist your feet somewhat to maintain your wedge. Use your sidestep and bullfighter maneuvers to climb uphill and repeat this in a glide until you're comfortable. A good instructor will be sure that the pitch (slope) you're on isn't too steep and that it's smooth enough for you to practice comfortably.

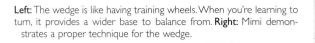

Left: The wedge is like having training wheels. When you're learning to turn, it provides a wider base to balance from. **Right:** Mimi demonstrates a proper technique for the wedge.

Every time you come down the pitch, you must get back up. After the first few practice runs, sidestepping gets tedious, and it's time to vary the approach. In the duck walk or herringbone you face up the slope, spread your ski tips apart, and use the inside edges of the skis to hold you in place. This is more rigorous than sidestepping, but it's faster if you're in shape.

If you're walking any distance up the slope, try taking your skis off and carrying them on your shoulder. Allow plenty of time to rest before you glide down again. Take your time and imagine yourself skiing while you hike to take advantage of the time spent in transit.

Many resorts have special lifts for the learning slopes to keep you from wasting too much energy going up each time. Handle tows are cables with handles that pull you up the slope. Other forms of surface lifts are *T-bars, J-bars, poma lifts,* and *rope tows.* T-bars accommodate two skiers at each position, J-bars and pomas only one. Rope tows are perhaps the oldest form of mechanical lift. If you're learning on one of these, be sure to wear old gloves or glove protectors, since gripping the rope directly can be tough on materials. T-bars, J-bars, and pomas are devices that are suspended from a moving cable that the skier holds onto while being propelled up the slope.

The newest form of skier transportation is a high-tech lift similar to the moving walkways in airports. You

THE CHAIRLIFT

When loading any chairlift, be sure to read the posted instructions. Lifts vary in make and design, even though they may look similar. Remember these guidelines.

- Hold your poles in your inside hand
- Wait for the signal from the operator
- Advance all the way to the marked load line
- Wait for the chair to touch the back of your knees before you sit
- Keep your skis parallel when sitting down
- Sit back and lower the restraint bar (if there is one; lifts in the western states often don't have restraint bars)

For unloading the chairlift,

- When approaching the unload area, check to be sure all clothing and equipment is free of the lift
- Raise the restraint bar at the Prepare to Unload sign
- Establish equal pressure on both skis as the chair reaches the unloading platform
- Push down on the chair with your free hand
- Rise off the chair as the platform begins to slope away
- Glide to the end of the runout and then move away quickly
- If you can't unload, keep your skis down and hit the stop wand
- Never jump from a chairlift under any circumstances: should the lift stop running, trained staff members will get you off

Top: Loading the chairlift. **Above:** Exiting the chairlift.

just stand on it, and it takes you up the hill. These conveyor belt lifts, sometimes called "magic carpets," are the ultimate in luxury for learners.

At some point during your many practice glides you'll probably fall—nature's way of helping you adjust your balance. Try to stay as relaxed as possible and to keep your hands ahead of your feet. Get up quickly to stay dry and out of the way of others who are learning.

There are many ways to get up from a fall, depending on your position on the ground. The best uses gravity to help you. First, get your behind on the uphill side of your feet, with your skis across the slope. Plant your poles in the snow close to you on your uphill side and use them as a lever to help you stand up. If this is too difficult you can remove one or both skis and replace them after you've recovered. Each time you go up and come down you'll gain confidence and maneuverability.

At the end of your first lesson, you'll probably be able to negotiate learning terrain by yourself. You'll have made your first direction changes and, if the learning slope at your resort has

Top: Getting up the hill can be arduous, but it provides valuable learning opportunities. You learn to use your edges and propel forward from your ankles, important skills as you progress. **Above left:** Karin and Tera take the "easy route" on a conveyor lift. **Above right:** Karin Sjostrom demonstrates proper tactics for riding a handle-tow.

one, tried a ski lift. For all practical purposes, you're now a skier!

"I couldn't believe it! I never thought I'd feel so comfortable! All my life I've watched my children and my husband do athletic things, and I've never been able to participate in any of them. After my very first time on skis I knew I'd found something I could share with them. Today I learned to turn and feel in control. I rode the learner's chairlift with my teenage son. I experienced beautiful views of mountains and trees, and I learned to control my speed and turns. I can't

Karin removes her skis to get up from the snow more easily.

wait for tomorrow!" After the first session, the emotions can be exhilarating for newcomers and coaches alike. Beverly was hooked after her first trip and found common ground with her athletic family.

WHAT COMES NEXT?

After the initiation comes the practice. Fortunately, practicing is fun. From now on all you'll do is practice! Every run you take and every turn you make will be practicing your skills and helping you ski better. The only catch is learning to practice effectively.

With repetition comes some inevitable regression in skill level. This a natural part of the sport. "It seems as though I need a few turns every weekend to get back into it," says Kim. "It seems easier to get going if I just roll with it and don't expect to be better and better. When I feel I'm not skiing my best, or not progressing in a lesson, I focus on what I'm truly enjoying at that moment, and I almost always feel better immediately." If you let yourself become frustrated, you can miss opportunities to improve or get past plateaus in learning. If you continue to stay within yourself and concentrate on what you want to do, potentially negative experiences such as falling, feeling out of control, or difficult conditions will remain in perspective.

Here's an example. If you're are learning to ski to be outside and enjoy the winter, does it truly matter if you fall on your second day? What would you be doing if you weren't here now? If you're learning because you want to ski with family or friends, remind yourself of the progress you've made. Remember what you were doing a day or an hour before. Log the plusses, then tackle the turns again. Focusing on why you're skiing becomes more and more important the longer you stay with the sport.

The second step to real success is to continue with a lesson program. You can look forward to gaining more effective control,

ADDITIONAL PRACTICE IDEA
• • • • • • • • • • • • • • • • • • • •

First, take off your skis and try running in arcs down a gentle slope. Then repeat the same arcs but shuffle your boots, never letting your feet leave the snow, so that a track forms. Now replace your skis and try to follow the tracks. In this exercise you're combining twisting movements of your feet with tipping movements that bring the skis' edges into play and help make cleaner turns.

Skiers with their pro, learning to shape a turn by shuffling in their boots.

These women are enjoying the crisp winter air at Sunday River, Maine.

Sometime during your first lesson, . . .
or during your second or third, . . .
you'll experience what you came for.
You'll glide down the shoulder of the
mountain, clean air on your face, and
encounter any one of a thousand
mountain views.

learning how to link your turns so you feel as if you're rhythmically dancing down the slope. You'll gradually use less and less effort and more and more finesse.

One lesson won't be enough to give you a true vision of where you can go as a skier. For your next learning experience, you must be even more particular. Be sure you are in charge of your learning, and let the teacher know why you're skiing, what your goals are, and what you've already accomplished. From there a good coach will help you define short-term goals that are attainable and will put you on a course toward reaching long-term ones. (See page 28.)

Sometime during your first lesson (if it's all day), or during your second or third, you'll get on a chairlift, and then you'll experience what you came for. You'll glide down the shoulder of the mountain, clean air on your face, and encounter any one of a thousand mountain views. The woodsy lushness of an eastern forest, the open grandeur of a Rocky Mountain paradise, the majestic western trees laden with snow—it's all within your reach.

Chapter 4

SKIERS' SURVIVAL SKILLS

YOUR RESPONSIBILITY CODE

1. Always stay in control, and be able to stop or avoid other people or objects.

2. People ahead of you have the right of way. It is your responsibility to avoid them.

3. You must not stop where you obstruct a trail, or are not visible from above.

4. Whenever starting downhill or merging into a trail, look uphill and yield to others.

5. Always use devices to help prevent runaway equipment.

6. Observe all posted signs and warnings. Keep off closed trails and out of closed areas.

7. Prior to using any lift, you must have the knowledge and ability to load, ride and unload safely.

This is a partial list. Be safety conscious.

KNOW THE CODE. IT'S YOUR RESPONSIBILITY

Now that you're on the mountain, it's important to under-stand how to move around safely. Learning to recognize common resort signs will help you get where you're going.

RULES OF THE ROAD

Now that you can ski under your own power, it's time to learn "Your Responsibility Code," a set of guidelines published by the National Ski Areas Association, similar to the rules of the road you follow when driving a vehicle. The code is very simple and mostly common sense, yet it's extremely important information for anyone new to the sport.

"Your Responsibility Code" is posted on numerous signs dotted around resorts. You might even see it on napkins and trail maps as friendly reminders.

• •

"**N**o sense being unprepared. Not much you can't face if you know it's coming."

—Mary, fifty-something, nurse

• •

• •

"**T**he image of that oncoming skier will be emblazoned in my mind forever! . . . I started off down the slope without looking up to see if anyone was coming. Thank goodness my coach was paying attention. She shouted, and the accident was avoided."

—Judy, age 30, bank officer

• •

1. Stay in control so that you can stop or avoid other people or objects.

2. Overtaking skiers or snowboarders have the responsibility for those in front of them.

3. Stop where you are visible from above and do not block a trail.

4. When entering a trail or starting off, look uphill and yield to oncoming skiers or snowboarders.

5. Always use retention devices (ski brakes or straps) to prevent runaway equipment.

6. Observe all posted signs and warnings. Stay off closed trails and out of closed areas.

7. Prior to using any lift, familiarize yourself with posted instructions regarding loading, riding, and unloading safely.

These rules are pretty basic, yet when you're overwhelmed with mountain scenery and other skiers and snowboarders zipping by, safety may not be uppermost in your mind. Remembering these simple rules will keep you skiing safely for years to come. Under the watchful eye of your coach, you'll learn the rules of the road experientially, as the situations are pointed out—yet another good reason to stay with a coach for at least your first few outings. "The image of that oncoming skier will be emblazoned in my mind forever!" exclaims Judy. "While I was practicing in a group lesson, I started off down the slope without looking up to see if anyone was coming. Thank goodness my coach was paying attention. She shouted, and the accident was avoided. I apologized and learned a valuable lesson!"

TRAIL SIGNS AND MAP USE

Ski resorts have standard signs. Just like international road signs, these signs are universal, and they will help you enjoy the parts of the resort you plan to visit and avoid the places you aren't ready for yet. Resort signs will also help you avoid danger zones, guide you to specific base areas, and help you locate your position on a trail map.

Ski runs are marked with signs indicating relative difficulty. Refer to resort trail maps or guides to find where you are on the mountain. This precaution will ensure that the runs you select will provide the experience you expect while taking you where you want to go.

green	blue	black	black	yellow
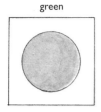	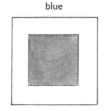		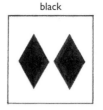	

Above: These signs appear as designations at the top of runs and on trail maps. Pay careful attention and plan routes of descent to be sure you can access the blues or greens all the way to the base of the mountain. **Right:** Blue runs are fun places to ski with friends. **Bottom right:** It's always a good idea to check the trail report before venturing out.

Runs marked with *green circles* are considered easier and are friendly enough for learners to enjoy after their first lessons. Even though several runs may be marked as "green" runs, they will all offer different challenges. Ask your ski teacher which of these runs would be best for your practice sessions.

Blue squares are considered more difficult and may be considerably steeper than the green runs. There may be mogul runs or longer, steeper faces on "blue" runs.

Black diamonds are considered the most difficult and are meant for advanced skiers and snowboarders only. These runs can be very steep and may contain sections of large bumps that can't be avoided. There are even more difficult runs known as double black diamonds.

Remember that the difficulty of any run can be altered dramatically by changing weather, grooming, and light conditions. Also, the size and spectrum of the resort may dictate the difficulty of its runs. Often runs designated as "blue" at a small resort in the Northeast would be similar to a "green" run at a larger western resort. Always check the trail report before venturing onto unfamiliar terrain. When in doubt, ask a pro.

Another important trail sign is the yellow caution sign, used if conditions on a run deteriorate or if there are dangers that aren't visible. Proceed slowly and carefully. Remember, in the mountains conditions change constantly. Resort staff could not possibly mark or draw attention to all hazards. Ultimately, getting around safely is your own responsibility.

STAYING SAFE AND COMFORTABLE IN THE MOUNTAINS

Baby, it's cold outside

It's not always cold at ski resorts, but even when it seems sunny and mild, mountains are notorious for changing temperatures. Mary, a fifty-something, stalwart Maine skier, has Reynaud's syndrome, which causes her extremities to lose circulation and get colder faster. "You'd think I shouldn't ski anymore, what with this circulation thing I've got. But they just keep getting more and more sophisticated clothing, and I just keep up with it. No sense being unprepared. Not much you can't face if you know it's coming."

Cold temperatures bring a couple of risks: frostbite and hypothermia. Both of these injuries can usually be avoided. Frostbite results when tissues freeze, causing serious damage much like that from a topical burn. Frostnip, the first indication of frostbite, is shown by whiteness of the skin. You may not feel it, so companions must watch each other for signs so the area can be warmed immediately. On frigid or windy days, make certain to cover all areas of skin. (See pages 28–31 for guidance on clothing.) The best treatment is prevention.

Hypothermia is defined by the core body temperature decreasing from the normal 98.6 degrees Fahrenheit to 91 or lower. Below 91 degrees, normal body functions are impaired, and a person may lose consciousness. The first sign of hypothermia is pronounced shivering. The condition can be avoided by dressing properly (especially covering the head, where large amounts of heat are lost; see page 30) and by movement. As a learner, you'll be using new muscle groups and practicing movements that will naturally keep you warm. Be aware of your body temperature, however, especially if it's particularly cold out or the wind is strong. If you feel chilled, let your ski teacher know. In a group it can be difficult to tell when individuals are getting cold, so be sure to sing out. A toasty mug of hot chocolate is a good way to ward off heat loss.

Sunshine on my shoulders

Snow magnifies the sun's rays, and overexposure can burn both skin and eyes. This danger is easily prevented with proper eye protection and sunscreen, but it's amazing how many people know the risks and still don't prepare. If the long-term risks of cancer aren't enough to get one's attention, the short-term effects of sunburn on the face and ears can be so severe from even a short exposure at high altitude that skiing may be impossible for many days. Retinal burns can also occur very quickly. The moral: Be sun sensible.

Eye protection is extremely important outdoors. Even on a cloudy day your eyes can be bombarded by ultraviolet rays, and wind and cold can also dry your eyes and make you uncomfortable. If it's cold, snowing, raining, or windy, goggles will protect your eyes. If it's sunny and warmer, sunglasses are a better choice. Seasoned skiers carry both. Glasses are easily stowed in a pocket when not in use, and goggles can be worn around the neck.

Both goggles and glasses come in a variety of lens colors. Choose yellow or amber for cloudy days, traditional dark lenses for sunny days. If you'll be skiing at night, clear lenses are best. If you want one all-purpose piece of protective eyewear, choose goggles with yellow lenses that have been treated for ultraviolet protection. Your eyesight is critical in skiing; be prepared and you'll see and ski much better.

Breathing thin air

If you're planning a skiing adventure that will take you to the high country such as the Rocky Mountains or the Sierra Nevada, be aware that acute mountain sickness (AMS) can occur in those not acclimated to the reduced oxygen levels found above six thousand feet. Though usually minor, AMS can cause distressing flulike symptoms. The best remedy is to get plenty of rest and avoid alcohol and caf-

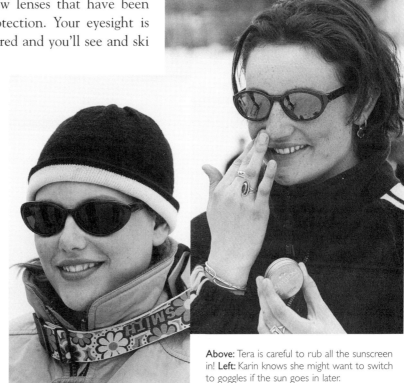

Above: Tera is careful to rub all the sunscreen in! **Left:** Karin knows she might want to switch to goggles if the sun goes in later.

feinated drinks, which can deplete your body of needed fluids. Luckily, most people adapt within twenty-four to forty-eight hours as long as they are prudent.

Mountain air can also be dry air, so you dehydrate faster. Bring water bottles, and drink as much water and juice as possible, even when you're not on the slopes. If you notice you're thirsty, you're already beginning to dehydrate. A slight headache is also a symptom, so heed the warning and drink up!

The increased vitality that fitness brings will definitely make your first ski experience more enjoyable. Skiing isn't a sport that gets you fit; it's a sport you enjoy more when you are fit.

GETTING FIT

While skiing is a wonderful opportunity to explore the winter environment, it is also a sport, and any sport requires some degree of fitness. You don't have to be as fit as the famous downhill racer Picabo Street to enjoy skiing, but it does help if you're active. In fact, as with any sport, the better your fitness level, the greater your chance of avoiding injury.

Preparing for your first experience

Your first time skiing may be when fitness most affects your performance. You'll be using new muscle groups and learning new movement patterns in an unfamiliar environment, causing more fatigue from stress and tension than when you've become more comfortable.

The best preparation for learning a new sport is an active lifestyle. If you already do things that increase your heart rate and work large muscle groups, such as tennis, bicycling, water skiing, running, in-line skating, or sailboarding, you're a step ahead. If you prefer a more formal workout, dance classes, aerobics classes, swimming, and other health club activities will work just as well. You need to get that heart rate up for at least twenty minutes three times a week.

If you don't currently have a workout regimen, try to begin one before learning to ski. The increased vitality that fitness brings will definitely make your first ski experience more enjoyable. Skiing isn't a sport that gets you fit; it's a sport you enjoy more when you are fit.

If you aren't particularly active, don't give up. With a just a little preparation you can get ready for your first time out, and perhaps this will motivate you to plan a regular fitness regimen. As you become a better skier, you'll want extra energy to take longer runs, ski later in the day, and tolerate more difficult conditions. For now, a few minutes of brisk walking each day (or a few trips up and down stairs) can boost your cardiovascular system, and a few additional activities will get you ready for your adventure.

Before starting any kind of exercise routine, especially if you're inactive, ask your physician about any limitations or any precautions you should take. When you're ready to begin, make sure you've warmed up with a few minutes of brisk movement such as jogging or a swift climb up the stairs. This will get the blood pumping to your arms and legs and lessen the chance of a pull or strain. Any recent publication on exercise and stretching will suggest specific warm-ups.

Next, practice the living room regimen in chapter 3 (pages 41–43). After doing the basic movements, practice them again more slowly and focus on controlling every movement. Next, practice moving from one foot to the other, pausing to balance on one foot. Work up to controlling the stance longer and longer. Be sure your body is lined up and that your knees are slightly flexed over your toes, arms out to the sides to help you. When this becomes easy, try it with your eyes closed.

The next step is to stand with hands on hips in the basic athletic stance. Close your eyes and slowly rock forward over your toes. Now rock back toward your heels. Then move back to center. Repeat, moving more and more slowly, and continually focus on finding the center.

Practicing indoor movements can increase balance.

MAINTAINING YOUR ENERGY

Carrying your ski equipment in an unruly armload can quickly deplete your energy, especially if you must walk any distance to the learning area. First, check to be sure your boots are buckled comfortably for walking. Some ski boots have a handy "walking mode" that makes it easier to travel in them. If you don't have this, just loosen the buckles a bit, yet not so much that you drag your heels. (See page 43 for how to carry your skis.)

Getting up from a fall can also take a lot of energy. If you've tried the techniques described in chapter 3 and still feel taxed, just snap off your bindings to get up easily. If the snow is sticky or deep, however, you may have trouble cleaning the bottom of your boots so you can get your bindings back on. Carry a snow scraper such as an old credit card in your pocket. This is a necessity on any deep snow day.

Finally, pace yourself comfortably. Take breaks, rehydrate, and refuel. If the others in your learning group are

Keeping a smile on your face is important!

slower or faster, ask to be placed in a different group. If you feel pushed, let your ski teacher know. Pros often teach beginning groups repeatedly, and they can miss signs of energy loss or frustration. They'll appreciate your letting them know how you're faring.

Now do the same exercise rocking laterally from one foot to the other and finding the center. These exercises will help you regain a centered stance while in motion on snow.

One area of the body that is often overlooked in skiing is the abdominal muscles. Your abs help bring you to center and hold you in balance as your legs work beneath you. The stronger your abs, the less stress on your lower back and the greater your enjoyment. Any good abdominal workout will suffice. You don't need washboard abs, but a little firming will go a long way.

Complete your initial workouts with some simple stretching that focuses on hamstrings, quadriceps, trunk, and back. As with all stretching, be careful and go slowly. Bouncing or forcing may pull something and set you back. Any good fitness routine includes stretching, and there are many resources out there.

Managing your energy for learning

The first step is to arrive at the resort rested. That means getting plenty of sleep the night before your adventure. If you're the type who'll worry and lose sleep because of nervousness, find out all you can up front. If you arrive a day early, you can take a tour, watch others learning, and perhaps even get your equipment fitted and ready to go. It may even be worth seeing if you can speak briefly with your coach. Just establishing contact will go a long way toward easing your anxiety. Consider talking with students from that day's session. Their excitement and enthusiasm will help get you geared up and in a state of mind to get the rest you need before it's your turn.

Another energy enhancer can be what you eat. Plan a good healthy breakfast. Oatmeal (if you like it) feels warm going down and stays with you. It's a great source of carbohydrates, which are easily converted to energy. And throughout the day, regularly drink all the water or juice you can hold.

Staying fit on a ski vacation

If you want to keep your regular fitness routine going while at the resort, you may need to do some research, but the opportunities are there. Many resorts are building health clubs that offer everything from lap pools to aerobics classes in the early morning and evening hours. Some on-slope lodgings have their own weight rooms and exercise equipment. Ask what's available when you make your reservation.

There's nothing finer than an early morning run around a ski resort. You'll get to see the resort waking up. Early morning sunlight through snow-laden branches is a fine inspiration for your day and will get your blood flowing. The biggest challenge to winter running is dressing appropriately and planning a route that you can complete easily at a run so you don't end up walking back and catching a chill. Be sure to plan on cooling down inside the gym or by walking through the hotel corridors. Ask resort personnel for suggested routes and distances, and be sure you have a map. Take it easy though—remember you're here to ski!

• •

"I think I kept taking lessons because I could practice without worrying about anyone else."

—Barb, age 39, librarian

• •

MAKING THE MOST OF PRACTICE TIME

A few years ago I had the pleasure of bringing Barb from cautious learner to confident explorer. Over a series of private lessons, we had more fun each time. She had two boys, ages seven and ten, who were beginning to want to ski more difficult terrain. Barb wanted to go with them but didn't want to keep them waiting. Her husband skied with a group of friends, but they usually left her on her own because she was intimidated by their speed as well. Barb had become more and more anxious and less and less adventuresome.

"I was having less fun, even though I realized that I knew how to ski. I wasn't really afraid, I was just cautious about trying new things and needed to set my own pace. Once I was able to try things without holding others up, I relaxed and enjoyed myself. I think that's why I kept taking lessons. It was my place to practice without worrying about anyone else. Then I could go back with the kids or ski with my husband's friends and enjoy the experience again."

A LEARNER'S GUIDE TO "SKI TALK"

. . . .

"When I started skiing I was so overwhelmed by the language that I just couldn't keep up with the terms that flew around the room. I felt so inadequate. As if I didn't belong and everyone knew it." These sentiments of an accomplished skier remembering her beginnings are not uncommon. It's hard, as an adult, to keep asking for explanations. Yet for the experienced skiers, it's hard to remember that what is common terminology for them is Greek to a new skier. Here's a simple guide to some of the terms you'll encounter at the resort.

angulation: Body movements that control the edge angle of the skis; edging. *See also* edge.

anterior cruciate ligament (ACL): A knee ligament susceptible to skiing injuries. The most talked-about injury for skiers of late is tearing the ACL. Much research is being done on treatment and rehabilitation, but the best treatment is prevention through basic leg strength and good instruction.

base: The bottom of the ski or the bottom of the resort (as in "base lodge"). "Base" can also refer to the current snow depth.

bevel: A tuning technique that enhances ski performance by making the edge differ from a ninety-degree angle.

bumps: *See* moguls.

camber: The amount of natural bend in the ski when it is placed on the ground. Your weight on the ski puts it into "reverse camber," helping to create a turn.

canting: Adjustments made to a ski to accommodate a skier's build and permit standing with the skis flat on the snow. Some boots claim to have canting adjustments, but this is an incorrect use of the term. What they do offer is the ability to align the cuff of the boot to the leg.

carved turns: Turns that utilize the skis' edges with little or no slipping.

(continued next page)

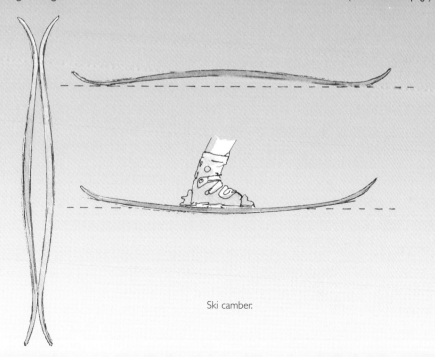

Ski camber.

A LEARNER'S GUIDE TO "SKI TALK"

• •

(continued from previous page)

detuning: Dulling the tips and tails of skis to avoid catching edges and make it easier to start a turn.

DIN: Deutsche industrie normen; a universal number manufacturers have agreed on to determine the point when bindings release. For example, a person who is five feet, five inches tall, weighs 115 pounds, and is an accomplished skier will have a DIN of 6. This will be the same no matter which binding company is used.

edge: The metal side of the ski, critical in the ski-snow relationship. Good skiers learn to control their edges by making "edge control movements," rolling the ski onto its edge so it can slice through the snow in a desired arc.

face: An open slope, often steeper than other parts of the run.

fall line: An imaginary line, commonly described as the path a ball would follow if released down a slope.

fat skis: New ski technology in ski design for those who want enhanced performance in powder snow. Wider than regular skis, they help prevent the skier from sinking into the snow.

garland: Scallops in the snow used to practice turns without actually completing a change in direction. A term used by ski teachers.

Geländesprung: A jump in which the legs are pulled up under the body. Old skiing lingo (German).

headwall: Open slope, usually much steeper than other parts of the run. *See also* face.

matching: Moving the skis so they are parallel during a turn.

moguls: Irregularities in the surface of the slope, usually caused by many skiers turning and pushing the snow into clumps that become more and more solid until they are bumps. Negotiating these surfaces with style and grace is a goal of many skiers. Mogul runs vary in steepness and difficulty, from relatively gentle and good for learning to extremely steep faces with moguls the size of refrigerators.

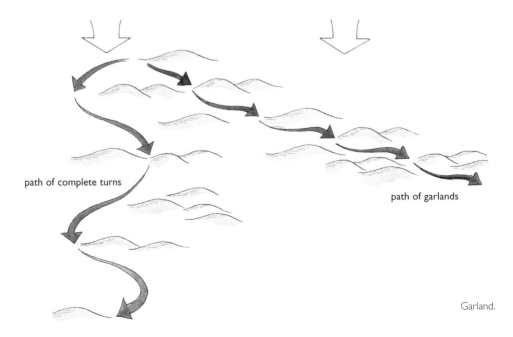

path of complete turns

path of garlands

Garland.

A LEARNER'S GUIDE TO "SKI TALK"

off piste: Areas of the ski resort not prepared or groomed. Sometimes these are open to the public, sometimes they are not, depending on weather and conditions or on the resort's resources for maintaining and patrolling them. These areas may be roped off, with a gate you can enter when open. *Piste* is a European term for a prepared ski run.

orthotic: A molded insert prescribed by a podiatrist or podorthist to correct and support the foot's position within a ski boot or other footwear. A true orthotic is built to measure. A more common insert, known as a footbed, can be made at most ski shops. Footbeds will support normal feet and improve the fit and comfort of the ski boots.

pressure: The force of a skier's weight while standing on skis is distributed over the bottom of the skis as pressure.

radius: Common reference to the size and shape of a turn, such as long-radius turns, medium-radius turns, and short-radius turns.

railed: A condition in which the ski's edges are raised above the base, detracting significantly from performance.

resort: Common name for a ski area.

roll: A movement used to get skis onto their edges, referred to as rolling the skis onto edge. *See also* edge.

run: The act of completing a trail or slope, as in "I'm going to make a run." Or a trail or slope, as in "That run is more difficult today than it was yesterday."

schussing: A German term for moving straight down the fall line.

shaped skis: Skis with greater sidecut than traditional skis.

sidecut: The characteristic of skis, when lying flat on the snow and viewed from above, to be wider at the tips and tails than in the middle.

sideslipping: Sliding down the slope with the skis crossways to the fall line. This maneuver is often used to negotiate difficult or challenging terrain.

Traditional skis (**left**) and shaped skis (**right**).

sitzmark: Old-fashioned term for the mark a skier leaves in falling.

skating: A movement like that done on skates, used by skiers to propel themselves on the flat or gain momentum.

ski brake: A device attached to the binding of the ski, designed to open when the ski releases. The prongs dig into the snow to prevent runaway skis.

snowplow: A position in which the ski tips are pointed toward each other and the inside edges are engaged to brake or turn. The snowplow is no longer used in modern ski teaching and has been replaced with wedge turns. Wedge connotes less braking and plowing action of the skis, more gliding and easier turning.

(continued next page)

A LEARNER'S GUIDE TO "SKI TALK"

• •

(continued from previous page)

stance: The way a skier stands on skis.

stem christie: A typical intermediate turn, somewhere between a wedge and a parallel turn. When correctly done, the outside ski moves on a continuous arc and the inside ski tip moves down the hill when the turn is begun.

stem turns: Turns begun by moving the uphill ski away, turning it, and then placing weight on it. Commonly thought to be an intermediate level of skiing, but an appropriate tool for any skier in some snow conditions.

tail: The rear of the ski.

telemark skiing: A variation on the theme; telemark is closer to the origin of skiing. Equipment has softer boots and bindings with a free heel similar to those used in cross-country skiing. However, telemark skis have metal edges meant to hold on steeper slopes. This type of skiing is most popular in back-country settings.

terrain park: A section of the slope that is often fenced off and contains "elements" that are built specifically for practice or play.

tip: The front of the ski. Also, a movement to engage the edge of the ski: "tip your ski onto its edge."

traverse: Skiing across the slope with no turn.

turn shape: The path the skis travel through a turn. The shape is adjusted to control speed and direction.

twist: A movement of the foot to aid in turning. "Twist the foot while you tip the ski onto its edge."

waist: The midsection of the ski.

wedge: A positioning of the skis in which they are on opposing edges. The wedge is often used as a tool to teach turning to beginners.

wedeln: A skiing style: swinging the rear of the skis from side to side while following the fall line (from the German, "wag"). Short swing was the next generation, and now good skiers are known for clean "short-radius" turns.

During my time with Barb, we identified her desire to ski comfortably with her boys and her husband. She is a reflective person, and as a librarian she spends a lot of time analyzing things. She enjoys hiking in the summer with her boys and her husband. "I enjoy hiking because of the beauty and peace I feel on the trail. There's plenty of time to think about how I climb something, or how I descend."

Barb and I explored as much terrain as we could during our lesson time. We didn't go to more and more difficult slopes; we simply picked different routes, played with speed, and looked for "little" adventures. The best time was the day we explored the "secret" trails the kids build. These are little woods trails that go on and off the beginner slopes. They have occasional bumps and twist and turn and wind back onto the regular trail. Barb was giggling so much that she forgot her hesitancy. "The kids' trails were fun! In some ways it was like being on a roller coaster, but I learned to control how fast I was going. After those trails, the open slopes seemed easier."

Next I took her to slopes that were a bit steeper and showed her how to negotiate them in control. By the time we'd completed four or five lessons, Barb had a different outlook on skiing. "Skiing used to come at me too fast, and I didn't have time to figure it out. During my lessons, I learned to plan how I wanted to ski a descent. That helped me to ski the way I hike: thoughtfully and in a way that allows me time to process everything. Now I have the confidence to go a bit faster and keep up with my family. The best part is the new places I've seen and the view from the top. Every run is a new adventure!"

Common problems

As you continue on your skiing adventure, there will inevitably be moments when you're unsure of the next step or even wonder if the adventure is worth the hassle and sometimes downright frustration. In any skill-based endeavor, practicing the right combination of skills in the right place at the right time for *you* is the only way to get better. Keep in mind the resources at your disposal. Though lessons, especially private ones, add initial expense, if you get the right coach the investment is invaluable. In fact it can save your vacation and your future on the slopes (see chapter 2).

Let's look at some typical complaints, their probable causes, and possible solutions. Put these thoughts to use, but always ask for a certified and experienced ski teacher to help before you give up.

"I get out of control more than I like"

Control is something that most skiers want more of but that the best skiers enjoy losing. In fact the real thrill in skiing comes from deliberately giving up control as you move from turn to turn. But that doesn't mean skiing totally out of control—quite the opposite. The best skiers move fluidly from turn to turn and regulate both speed and direction.

Control begins with understanding turn shapes—how to create a path from turn to turn that will produce a comfortable speed. Look at the shapes in the diagram. The first shows a path with very narrow turns. Imagine a marble following a groove down a tilted tray. It would gain

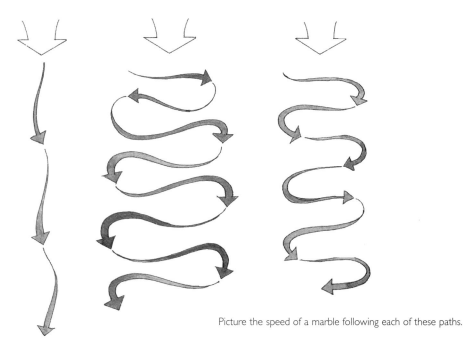

Picture the speed of a marble following each of these paths.

speed as it progressed to the bottom. In the second path, with wider turns, the marble would lose momentum and almost stop between turns, depending on the steepness of the slope. The third path would offer a constant speed down the tray.

It's also clear that the more steeply the tray is tilted, the more like the middle path the grooves would have to be to keep the marble at the same speed. Your skis behave the same way on the side of a mountain. As the slope becomes steeper, add more "shape" to your turn to maintain speed.

Notice also that the grooves in the diagram are always curved. This is a secret to good skiing as well. Most learners think of turns as something to do when they get across the slope and need to get back. Good skiers are always turning; their skis are always scribing an arc. In this manner the ski can be used as a tool, and it can be on edge most of the time. Staying balanced over the edge of the ski means having more control.

Above: The author in the arc of her own choosing. **Right and below:** Letting go of the old turn (**A**), moving into the new one (**B**), and voilà (**C**)—complete!

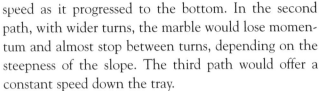

Learners make the mistake of using a turn only to change direction, usually to avoid other skiers or the trees on the side of the trail. This causes them to take the first path on page 63. They suddenly twist the skis to the other direction (usually with added twisting of the upper body, just to make sure), causing the edge to lose its grip on the snow and slide sideways. The steeper the slope and the harder the snow surface, the more likely the skis are to slip out of control.

Good skiers take the second path in the diagram. When you make a smooth and continuous turn, the skis' edges can maintain their grip on the snow through the turn. You do this by looking farther along the desired path so that the skis are guided continuously, not twisted quickly at the last minute. You probably practice this skill when driving your car. Looking down the road toward possible obstacles allows you the reaction time to turn or stop the vehicle smoothly. Good skiers look ahead and plan direction changes, allowing the skis to maintain their course and stay in control.

Remember, though, that control is maintained in the instant you lose it. Even good skiers can misjudge how early to begin the next turn and hang onto the old one just a bit too long. The result is a quick move at the last second and a momentary loss of grip on the snow. Experience and coaching will help you learn when to let go of the old turn and move freely toward the next one.

"I don't like ice"

Most skiers associate ice with noise under their skis and a sudden slide sideways, bringing loss of control or even a fall. Even the best skiers are challenged when the snow surface becomes polished.

The difficulty on ice usually occurs when you turn. You feel the ice under you, panic, and do what you think will slow you down—turn. Unfortunately the quick, panic-driven turn causes the skis to lose their grip, causing you to slide and lose control.

The first remedy is to avoid turning on the ice. There's usually plenty of snow above and below an icy patch (which is created by skiers repeatedly turning in the same spot). Look for the

snow and turn there. It's a simple remedy, but difficult unless you're confident enough to look for the good snow.

There are times when you can't see the ice ahead, and the sensation suddenly changes, as does the sound your skis make. Most skiers, as in the example above, panic and twist the skis, causing even more problems. When you feel the snow change, you can simply adjust your course to ski across the ice and turn in the snow on the other side. This requires you to be agile and balanced and to think quickly. Practice is the key. A good coach will help you practice on flatter slopes that offer less than perfect conditions. Imagine the boost you'll feel when you can be challenged rather than intimidated by hard snow!

"Bumps, even soft ones that appear at the end of the day, intimidate me"

Moguls are a skier's playground, yet bumps are probably the biggest hurdle skiers face. Somehow, little children see them for what they are: the unex-

Above right: This group of women are happily looking for "good snow."
Right: Karin studies her options.

The author moving forward and absorbing the moguls to retain balance (**A–D**). A close-up of "absorbing" a bump (**E–J**). Note the active movement toward the bump and active retraction of the legs under the body as the bump is negotiated. Particularly note the extension of the legs as the bump becomes a thing of the past. The legs are long again and ready for the next bump.

·pected, the break from the ordinary, the difference that can make you giggle and surprise yourself. We adults, however, in our quest for control and for grace on the snow, tend to be easily discouraged.

To understand why moguls challenge even veteran skiers, look at the shape of the bump itself. When your skis slide up the bump, unless you actively move your body forward, inertia tilts your mass back and you lose your balance. Compound that by what happens when the skis crest the top of the bump and slide down the back side. This is where gravity and momentum rear their ugly heads, causing the skier to get even farther behind the movement of the skis and feet. It can feel like being squeezed from a tube of toothpaste and splattering on the bristles of the toothbrush!

To avoid being splattered, find a section of small bumps or rolls (terrain parks often have a series of rolls that are excellent for this) on gentle terrain. Practice actively moving your body forward while flexing your legs to allow your feet and skis to slide up the front

Above left: Karin forgot to move forward over the bump. . . . **Left:** Tera gets left behind, too. As a result, she must overcompensate on the other side and sacrifice balance. The next few moguls will no doubt continue the bucking-bronco ride.

Right: Four approaches to a mogul slope. **(A)** Zipper line: this line merely "deflects" from bump to bump and increases speed. While fun for pros, this line isn't the way to go while you're learning. **(B)** Representing a more moderate approach, this line shows how turns can be shaped around the moguls to maintain speed. Notice the turns happen on the tops and sides of the moguls rather than in the ruts or troughs (as in line A). **(C)** Another moderate approach, the line here is a little more aggressive than line B but still uses the tops and sides of the moguls, where there is more snow. **(D)** This is a long line, good for finding the friendly Vs and for practicing absorbing the undulating terrain.

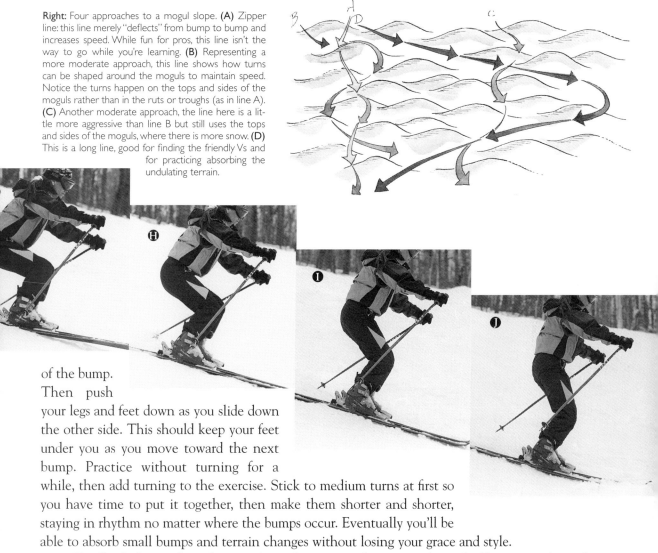

of the bump.

Then push your legs and feet down as you slide down the other side. This should keep your feet under you as you move toward the next bump. Practice without turning for a while, then add turning to the exercise. Stick to medium turns at first so you have time to put it together, then make them shorter and shorter, staying in rhythm no matter where the bumps occur. Eventually you'll be able to absorb small bumps and terrain changes without losing your grace and style.

Finally, find a good coach to teach you how to "read" a series of moguls. Skiing moguls can be a lot like paddling a canoe through whitewater. You learn to look for the "friendly Vs" so you can avoid the rocks in a river. Similarly, you learn to look for the "friendly turning zones" on different shapes and sizes and combinations of moguls.

"If there are even a couple of inches of new snow, rather than being excited like everyone else, I just get tired and flail"

When fresh snow falls, it seems people are ecstatic at first but soon tire and have a difficult time. This is because your skis are *in* the snow rather than *on* the snow. There's a great physical difference between skiing through something and skiing over it.

Skiing *in* snow can also require caution, depending on the terrain. **Inset:** Skiing in snow provides new and different sensations, opening up a new array of challenges.

The first problem with skiing *in* snow is that there's more resistance around your feet. This drag varies with the texture of the new snow. The less consistent and predictable it is, the harder it is to stay balanced. Add terrain inconsistencies under the snow, and the difficulty is doubled.

Begin to face the challenge by learning about the snow that has fallen on any particular day. In colder temperatures the snow is likely to be more consistent and predictable yet will just cover any impediments lurking beneath it, such as an icy patch or a bump. In warmer temperatures the snow will stick together more, creating more suction on the surface of the skis and a sensation of build-up and release that can throw you off balance.

Once you have a sense of the snow type, work to feel your balance point as you turn (see page 69, top). If you feel the snow pushing your feet back, pull them forward to regain equilibrium. If you feel your feet getting ahead of you, try to pull them back under you.

Once you can feel and adjust to the snow's pull and tug, focus on your turn shape and rhythm. Try to maintain an even, round turn. The deeper the snow,

This skier lost balance as her skis moved through a pile of slushy snow.

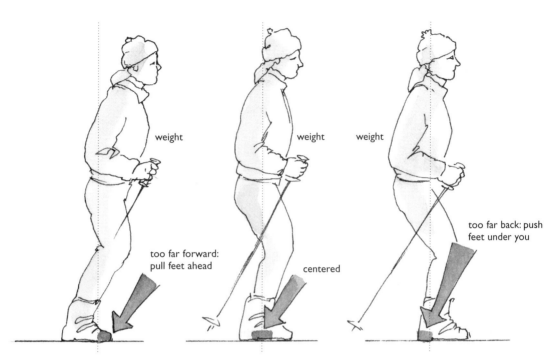

weight

weight

weight

too far forward:
pull feet ahead

centered

too far back: push
feet under you

Above: Finding your balance zone in powder. **Right:** Skiing in deep snow often feels like bouncing on a trampoline.

the more your legs will need to pull up under you and then reach toward the ground. When the rhythm gets going, you may feel as if you're bouncing on a trampoline as you pull and push your legs through the turns. Once the rhythm is established, momentum will almost pull you from turn to turn, making your skiing feel less like aerobics class and more like floating. (Of course this depends on how light the snow is.) Practice on a moderate slope where you can feel momentum but aren't threatened, then step it up as you become more comfortable.

Chapter 5

WHO SHARES YOUR ADVENTURE?

Nothing can replace the friendships made on the slopes.

Here I was with someone I loved, enjoying the winter and feeling more alive than I ever dreamed possible.

"There was a time when I went skiing in college with a group of friends," Kim remembers. "We'd planned the trip for a long time and were really excited to go. When the day arrived it was cold and windy, and the forecast was even worse. When we got to the resort, one of the gals began to grumble about the weather. Her negativity was catching, and soon everyone was getting cold and miserable. We quit skiing early and left discouraged. I don't think I even went skiing again the rest of that season.

"The next year I met a woman in one of my classes who was a skier. We talked about it and decided to go skiing together. We laughed and giggled the whole way to the resort. We decided to take a workshop to help orient us to the mountain, and we ended up skipping classes to stay longer than we'd planned. The kicker is, the weather was not a factor! It just didn't matter, because

> "The weather . . . just didn't matter, because we enjoyed each other's company."
>
> —Kim, age 40, nurse practitioner

we enjoyed each other's company. We explored everything we could at the resort, and the positive interaction between us kept our spirits high."

SKIING WITH A FRIEND

When it comes to skiing, pick your friends carefully. Be aware that differences in skiing ability can really change the experience. If you're going to a resort with people who've skied all their lives, beware. A lot of details that a lifelong skier takes for granted can overwhelm a newcomer to the sport.

"I brought a new boyfriend skiing, and it was the beginning of the end of our relationship!" Jan met Matt at summer school and invited him to go skiing with her the next winter. He'd never skied before, but he was athletic and excited about trying. Jan remembers the scene at the resort. "I was overwhelmed by all the things a new skier has to do. I tried to help him get it together, but I quickly got frustrated and cranky. I left him in his lesson and finally got to make some turns, although I was alone. When I met him at the end of his lesson, I wasn't very appreciative of his new skill. I wanted to go up the mountain, but I realized that Matt wasn't going to be able to come with me for a while. Instead of encouraging him and having fun where he was, I got impatient and sullen. Needless to say, Matt never skied again, and I soon stopped seeing him altogether."

The only way Jan could have made this story worse would have been to try to teach Matt herself! Friends can totally make or break your experience. If you're a new skier, try to go either with someone who will learn the ropes with you in good humor or with someone who already knows the ropes and will be patient while you learn them. If you expect a friend who is an accomplished skier to "set you up," you may be disappointed. If Jan had thought about what she was getting into as a sponsor, she and Matt might have had a different experience.

When the emotional mix is right, you can enhance not only your skiing experience, but your friendship. Mermer remembers a day of deep snow and sunshine at a western resort a few years ago. "There we were, the two of us, looking out over this seemingly endless expanse of white. We had hiked over a ridge and come out on the edge of a bowl that hadn't yet been skied. It was very steep,

> " . . . Needless to say, Matt never skied again, and I soon stopped seeing him altogether."
>
> —Jan, age 18, student

Challenge enhances the sense of camaraderie.

and my stomach was churning. I had skied things as steep or steeper many times, and so had she, but just looking down can assault the senses. At that moment we looked at each other and grinned. The rest of the day we were literally playing in the snow together, initial nerves forgotten. Now, whenever I think of her, I remember that grin and that moment."

HOW TO SKI WITH YOUR FAMILY AND STILL LOVE THEM

One of my least favorite days skiing with my family happened when I forgot that family needs multiply in a strange place. I brought my two children, ages five and six, to a new resort for a day of business and, I hoped, family time. Since I wasn't familiar with the ski area, I found I couldn't provide adequately for their needs. I arrived later than planned and had to walk—carrying my gear, my kids' gear, and at some points my kids—through two parking lots that angled steeply toward the base area. I didn't know there was a shuttle, so I arrived with two unhappy children and an aching back. I didn't know where various services were, including the kids' programs, so I had to search them out while my children whined and cried. I got the same looks I remembered from the grocery store. You know—people think you're an abuser when all you've done is ask your child not to scream and throw things (for all the good *that* does!).

I finally found the children's center, but the morning session had already begun. Luckily the program manager took pity on me and offered to place my children anyway. I blessed her and ran off to my meeting, more than an hour late. By the time the day was over we were all exhausted. The drive home was the best part of the trip, because the kids fell asleep and I knew the way. I still have bad memories of that resort, but it all could have been avoided If I'd done a bit of planning.

Yet skiing with my children has provided other memories that I'll treasure as long as I live. I still remember my son's first turns, the first time my daughter made it through a race course, and our first family vacation at a western resort. Skiing has given my children something positive to focus on in their preadolescent and teenage years. It's furnished them with a social outlet both with peers and with adults. But mostly it's been a way to play together, a source of common ground and much family laughter.

So how do you participate as a family? The first step involves planning. Do your homework so you're ready both physically and emotionally for the resort experience.

Getting there

First of all, be sure you have correct directions to the resort and know how much time to allow for driving or taking other transportation. If you take a shuttle from a

A typical unloading scene.

hotel, be sure you know how long it will take. Most shuttles make stops along the way, which can affect your plans.

Get a map of the base area of the resort and be sure all the services you need are clearly marked. You'll need to plan the route from your car or shuttle to each step along the way. Call ahead to see if there's an unloading zone, especially if you have children to enroll in programs or a lot of gear to carry.

Dressing children for success

Most parents have the same goal when introducing their children to skiing: they want them to have an enjoyable experience that they'll be eager to repeat. When preparing your child for a day of skiing, some tricks of the trade will help you attain the goal of fun and comfort. The best ski program in the country can be an ordeal if a child is cold and miserable.

The best ski program in the country can be an ordeal if a child is cold and miserable.

Just as for adults, the first principle in dressing children for the weather is to layer their clothing. Begin with polypropylene long underwear, both bottoms and tops, which is designed to breathe and wick moisture away from the skin. Next add a turtleneck and light sweatpants (not jeans, since they can bind and be hard to move around in). Follow that with a sweater, preferably wool or a wool blend that will keep heat in. When choosing a parka and outer pants, look for designs that permit a full range of movement and allow for growing room yet are not so large that they are cumbersome. Waterproofing is essential, since your child will be on or near the ground often, especially at first. Be sure there's adequate insulation for the climate. Children get cold more easily than adults because they have less insulating body fat. And small

Your child will enjoy the experience more if properly dressed.

children don't notice they're getting cold—they just suddenly *are* cold. Be sure the outer layers aren't too slippery, to avoid a long slide after a fall and reduce the risk of slipping off a chairlift.

Socks are particularly important, since they affect both the fit of the ski boot and the warmth of the toes. Wearing more than one pair of socks, or socks with ribbing on the ankles—common in children's socks—can cause discomfort and even frostbite because the socks bunch up and cut off circulation. One pair of polypropylene and wool blend socks designed for skiing can help keep the cold toes blues at bay.

Mittens and gloves are primary, since a beginner's hands are continually on or near the snow. More experienced children must be able to hold ski poles and keep their hands warm while on lifts and long runs. Mittens are best for small children and beginners, since they tend to be warmer. They absolutely *must* be waterproof and windproof. Some brands now come with built-

Far left: Helmets add comfort for parents as well as children. **Left:** Many kids' sunglasses don't provide UV protection. Be sure to check the label.

in pockets for handwarmers that last up to seven hours. But the warmest mittens or gloves won't help unless your child can easily get them on or off and use his or her hands easily with them on. To avoiding losing them, you can attach the mittens to the child's parka with small clips.

The easiest neck protection for a child is a gaiter. They come in colors to match almost any ski outfit and in soft materials to protect delicate skin. Children can put them on by themselves, and you needn't worry about a scarf's getting caught in a lift. The same thing goes when choosing a hat. The stocking caps that have become popular are cute, but they can get caught in a chairlift. Further, the hat should be warm yet not block vision or hearing. Be sure to tie or tuck up long hair as well.

A helmet adds safety as well as warmth. Modern helmets for kids have good ventilation and let them hear. They're lightweight and often extremely fashionable.

Protection for the eyes is essential. Ultraviolet rays can severely damage a child's eyes, as can strong winds, and the discomfort can detract from the fun. On cold, overcast, or windy days, children should wear goggles of the correct size. Look for lenses that don't block peripheral vision and that feel comfortable on the cheeks and nose. On bright days sunglasses are appropriate as long as your child will wear them. Put them on a neck strap and be sure they fit your child's face. Of course, be sure they furnish enough UV protection.

The sun can also take its toll on unprotected skin. Be sure your child wears sunblock. Remember that even on a cloudy day ultraviolet rays can be a problem, especially when reflected from the snow. Wind is also hard on a child's delicate skin, and many face creams are thick enough to protect from wind as well as sun.

When children are properly prepared, it's much easier to enjoy the slopes and the activity.

When you've accumulated all the clothing your child will need to stay warm and comfortable and protected from the elements, you may want to take time to label everything with your child's name. In a busy ski school small items like mittens and goggles can easily get separated from their owners, to parents' distress and expense. It's also wise to bring along extra socks, mittens, goggles, and hat in case something gets wet or is lost.

When comfortably and warmly dressed, your child is ready to explore the winter playground.

Let's get going!

Get very young children out of bed much earlier than you think necessary. They always take more time than planned eating and dressing and loading into the car. (Make sure they do eat!) Let them know what to expect. If they're three or older, talk to them about walking by themselves, carrying items, and most important, the fun they can expect. (Three-year-olds like to help, so plan what small items they can realistically carry. This will help them to feel part of it all and to do what you need most—get themselves there!) Even children who go to day care can look forward to having fun in the snow and doing something new.

Talk to your children about ski school, and let them know that you won't be staying with them. Even children who are used to being in day care or kindergarten may think a family vacation means you'll be with them the whole time, and this misunderstanding can cause great distress. Try to show them photos of where they'll be and of children learning to ski.

Call ahead to ask how busy the staff predict the day will be and to see if you can complete any procedures ahead of time. At some resorts you can visit the children's center the night before to register and let your child meet the staff.

Finding a good kids' program

When introducing your child to skiing, the main goals are *safety*, *fun*, and *learning*, in that order. You must assure yourself that all reasonable precautions have been taken for your child's safety, that the emphasis is on creating an exciting and rewarding experience that your child will want to repeat, and that the teaching is outcome oriented. Here are some things to consider when choosing a ski school. Be sure to call ahead with specific questions, and decide whether the program will meet your needs. Keep in mind that you're on vacation, and careful planning can help you avoid unpleasant surprises.

> "They sent me off with a pager in case things got ugly. When I returned an hour or so later, Jamie was happily practicing his 'pizza' skills. . . . I was so impressed to find a happy child and an obviously prepared staff!"
>
> —Kim, age 40, nurse practitioner

First consider the program itself. Are there reservations? What ages are accepted? Some programs operate only on weekends and holidays, so be sure to ask when lessons are available. Ask what's included in the price. A lift ticket? Lunch? Supervision? Video? It's hard for a twelve-year-old to be grouped with five- and six-year-olds, just as you would probably be unhappy learning with

Karin, a seasoned children's teacher, enjoys her small charges, while mom enjoys the slopes elsewhere!

small children, so if you have older children, be sure to ask how the classes are split. By age, ability, or both? Ask about instructor/child ratios. Be wary of groups larger than ten children. Three-year-olds do not function well in large groups or in all-day programs, so find out what allowances they make for a small child's needs. Additionally, many areas require security checks before small children can be picked up. Inquire about this if it's a concern. And finally, find out what extras are available such as after-hours child care, "kids' night out" or special programs such as "race day," "teddy bear day," and other events that make a vacation special for kids *and* their parents.

It's also a good idea to get a feel for the physical plant. Where are the buildings located on the ski area property? Are they near where the children will be skiing? Is the learning area enclosed and protected from the skiing public? Are there food service and bathrooms near the children's skiing area? How easy is it for them to get there when they're outside? Are there lifts just for the kids in the program, or specially designed lifts? Small children tire easily and will need special provisions for lift riding. Are there slopes that will challenge more advanced kids and excite them without forcing them onto difficult terrain too quickly? Many ski areas are now building mountain "adventure zones" for children that incorporate structures they can learn and play on. This stimulates learning and fun without encouraging them to tackle slopes that are too difficult. It also creates a place just for them that challenges and excites them in a creative and safe way.

"I got a day off from work on the spur of the moment, and I brought my four-year-old to the resort with me." Kim remembers a particularly trying day for her child. "Jamie was difficult to awaken and was cranky all morning. He'd been skiing before and was excited about going again, but he was just having a bad day. When I dropped him off, I tipped off his instructor and reluctantly left him, teary-eyed, standing by the door. I just wanted to make a few runs, and I let the staff know I'd check on Jamie to see if it was going to work. They sent me off with a pager in case things got ugly. When I returned an hour or so later, Jamie was happily practicing his 'pizza' [wedge] skills. I noticed he had on a different outfit, and I sneaked in the back door to find out why. When I found Evelyn, the supervisor, she explained that Jamie had spilled hot chocolate all over his outer clothing. They'd thrown everything into the laundry, and Jamie was in an extra outfit they kept on hand for just such occasions. I was so impressed to find a happy child and an obviously prepared staff!"

All the fancy facilities and programs in the world mean little without a well-trained, caring staff. It's the little things that matter. Be sure that your children will be enjoyed by folks specially trained to meet their needs. A good ski school program will create wonderful memories for your child. Choose with care and you'll be rewarded with a family sport that will provide excitement and joy for years to come.

Making sure your teens are happy

Now that my children are older, I still occasionally take them with me when I travel to other resorts on business. On one such trip we discovered that teenagers need special services that many resorts don't provide. My kids were thrilled with the skiing experience, yet in the evening, when we adults were content to relax by the fireplace, they were pacing the floors and complaining that they had nothing to do.

Look for resort services such as teen clubs, movie theaters, and health clubs that offer specific activities where teens can meet each other and do things. I ended up driving long distances to find entertainment for my teens when I much would have preferred to hand over that detail.

Be sure you allow your teens the option of skiing with other teens and not spending the whole day or vacation in your company. As appealing as this may sound as family time, letting them be apart from you will make the time you do spend together truly worthwhile.

What about your spouse?

If your spouse is at the same ability level as you are, you're one of a blessed few. The usual case is that one partner skis a good deal better, and the "slope wars" are on. It seems that one either gets pushed beyond the comfort level or has to stay on the lower mountain. If this is so, check into taking group classes where you'll be grouped with others of similar ability and perhaps meet some folks to share your runs.

Top: Tera and Mimi have a special relationship. **Above:** Women enrolled in Women's Turn at Sunday River in Bethel, Maine.

Skiing together

When I was a child my parents belonged to a group of friends who skied together every weekend. As we grew, we got used to having a couple of runs with the family and then branching off to ski with the friends each of us had chosen. Now my children do the same.

Skiing with your children can be the most fun you have at the resort, or it can be the hardest thing you do. It all depends on how you handle it. If you're not an accomplished skier yourself, never attempt to bring a very young child skiing with you. Better to place kids in a good-quality program, as described above, and set about learning yourself. When you *both* are capable of skiing down gentle slopes under your own power, then it's time to venture out together. Ask the instructor thoughtful questions about your child's progress. Be sure you don't get in over your head—one scary experience can ruin the sport for you and your child. Some resorts offer private lessons for very small children along with their parents. The instructor will get to know both of you and show you how to ride lifts with your children and how to motivate them with games and activities that will keep them happy, interested, and most important, learning to ski independently.

Never take your child's familiarity with a lift for granted.

GETTING CHILDREN UP THE MOUNTAIN

There's nothing natural about riding a ski lift, and it should be treated with the same healthy respect as any other motorized device. Most problems in skiing with children concern lifts. Before considering using the lift, be sure children can sidestep or duck walk up a small hill, do a straight run, and turn to a stop (see pages 44–45). Then, by the time they ride the lift they have some control over their skis.

Never take your child's familiarity with a lift for granted. This is one area where constant reminders and repetition of instructions are necessary. Stress paying attention when loading and unloading from a lift, but without frightening your child. Operators on beginner lifts are usually trained to load children. Here are suggestions for different types of lifts you may encounter.

1. **Handle tows or rope tows.** Have children practice by holding on to a rope while you pull them a short distance so they can get the feel of sliding and being pulled. The child needs to practice grabbing the rope, standing up as it pulls, and letting go at the top. For very young children this is usually difficult at first. Stand right behind them, grab the handle or rope, and let yourself begin to be pulled with your child between your legs. Be extremely careful that your child's skis don't get lodged under yours, which can cause serious falls. If you're not sure you can manage your child in this way, don't try: you may be in for knee injuries or worse. Once your child is holding on sufficiently, gradually move back. Both your child and you should look ahead and keep your skis straight. If necessary, let go, but be sure to move quickly away from the rope so

as not to interfere with others following. If the unloading area at the top is not level, be ready to help your child unload.

2. **Poma lifts.** For poma lifts, practice with a simulated poma made from a frisbee attached to a mop handle. Have your child practice walking up and positioning the skis uphill, then place the poma between the legs, pretending to ride. Be sure children understand that they cannot sit down. After their "ride," practice taking the poma from between their legs and handing it off (see illustration at right).

Practice removing the poma.

3. **T-bars.** T-bars are much like poma lifts, but they can be more difficult to ride since they are made for two people, and both must keep their skis straight and balance the T evenly. This is difficult when people of different heights ride the lift together. Many adults bring very small children up on the T-bar between their own skis. Though this is relatively efficient for a strong person who is an accomplished skier, it can be dangerous if skis get tangled or any irregularities appear in the track. In addition, if you must let go of the lift, it can swing and hit a child in the head. Children should practice taking the T-bar, properly positioning themselves on the lift, and then getting off or releasing the lift. Emphasize holding poles in the outside hand, looking over the other shoulder, and reaching for the shaft with the hand closest to you. Try to spend time on the flat holding a mock T-bar between you. This will help children realize that riding a T-bar is definitely a joint effort. They should stand up and keep their knees slightly bent. One of the most common mistakes first-time T-bar riders make is to sit on the bar. This bar is meant to be placed just below your rear; it is not a seat. If you are riding next to a small child, the bar might have to be as low as your knees to be comfortable for the child. Remind children that if they lean to the side or don't pay attention they may fall off. They must also be prepared to let the bar swing free at the top or hand it to the attendant.

4. **Chairlifts.** Some resorts have practice chairlifts, but don't expect it. If not, spend time watching the loading procedure. Describe how to unload, and be sure your child understands what's going on. Since falling off a chairlift can be far more serious than falling off a poma, safety can hardly be overemphasized.

MOMMY, LET GO!

• • • • • • • • • • • • • • • •

I've been earning a living as a ski teacher since I was twenty years old. All through my child-bearing years I taught skiing, mostly so I could introduce my children to the sport. One sunny afternoon I was able to retrieve my children from day care and bring them both out-side with me. My daughter Karin was just three years old and able to ski by herself, and my son Josh was two, still dependent on me to hold him over his skis. This would be the first day I'd taken them out together, so Josh had never seen his sister ski.

When we arrived at the top of the slope, Karin pushed off. At this moment Josh was gliding along between my skis, with me holding him. He heard Karin exclaim "Here I go!" and looked over to see her swoop down the trail. He paused a moment, looked up at me, and shouted "Mommy, let go!" He pushed out from between my legs with his little arms, and off he went. At first I was afraid he wouldn't be able to stop, but it was soon apparent that it had just never occurred to him that he could do it by himself. He had all the skill; he just hadn't been motivated. When he

(continued next page)

Above: This cheery group is waving to get the attendant to slow the lift for exit.
Right: Exiting the lift is simple when you're prepared.

Before entering the loading area, ask the lift attendant to help you or to slow the lift. As you line up, be sure the child understands not to make a wedge when loading, which can make the skis cross with yours and cause falls. Hold the child's poles with your own in your outside hand (if you're carrying them) and reach around the child's waist with your other arm. Depending on the height of the chair, you may need to lift the child onto the seat and to the back as you close the safety bar. Do not let go until the child is settled and not likely to wiggle free and perhaps slide out of the seat. While riding, warn against clicking the skis together, which might release the bindings. Also, slippery pants might let a child slide out. Keep your poles across the child's lap just in case. Near the top, watch for the Prepare to Unload sign, and tell your child to hold on while you carefully raise the bar and not to slide forward until you are just reaching the unloading area. You may need to lift your child down, since a child's short legs may not reach the unloading ramp. Watch for a designated spot where your feet should touch down, then help your child off. Again, stress keeping the skis parallel so as not to cross with riding partners' skis. You and your child should glide to a natural stop well away from the ramp. If you have trouble, wave to the top attendant for help. If you are considering letting your child ride a chairlift with other children, note that, should the lift need to be evacuated, they must be old enough to take direction from the ski patrol and to wait for help. Many resorts will not allow children under age seven to ride with other children.

5. **Gondolas.** Since both gondolas and trams are loaded and unloaded by attendants, you don't need to spend much time practicing. Be sure to explain to children that they are to hand their skis to the attendant (or take them inside if they are very small). Stress sitting or standing quietly and paying attention. Some children may be afraid of the gondola, since they might ride with strangers or not be able to see out the windows. If you're on a tramway car where you have to stand up, be aware that your child's view may be of people's zippers and boot tops. Try to enter the car early and get a window seat. If this is impossible, stay close to your child. Unloading must be fairly quick, so be sure you're ready to get off and that your child knows what direction to go afterward.

MOMMY, LET GO!
• • • • • • • • • • • • • • • •

(continued from previous page) saw his sister skiing, he took off! I watched from a distance, tears streaming down my cheeks, realizing this was just one of many steps toward independence my children would take.

We went back to the chairlift for a second ride. On the ride up Josh fell fast asleep, and I carried him down, my heart aching with love and with appreciation of the day and the shared moment.

Riding the chairlift can provide a welcome break. Some children even fall asleep!

SKIING WITH YOUR UNBORN CHILD

Many women shy away from skiing when pregnant. During my second pregnancy I skied almost until the end, and I truly enjoyed getting outside and being active. Not only did it keep me healthier in mind and spirit, but the exercise kept me in shape for the big event. Consider these points.

- **Balance.** The changing shape of your body changes your balance. As long as you stay active you'll adapt, but if you don't ski for a long time you'll need a longer warm-up.

- **Flexibility.** Your body gets ready for childbirth by becoming more flexible, so it takes more strength to keep your joints lined up. Many pregnant women complain of lower back pain and other aches because of this. As with balancing, if you ski regularly throughout your pregnancy it should be less of an issue.

- **Falls and injuries.** Your baby is extremely well protected against small bumps and falls, but when you're pregnant even a sprain or strain can present problems for you.

- **Other skiers.** Collisions with other skiers are probably the highest risk during pregnancy. You can control your own actions but not those of other skiers. It's best to ski during less busy times and stick to trails that offer high visibility.

As with any activity during pregnancy, consult your physician and agree on a well thought out plan.

APPRECIATION

A few years ago, I was skiing with my husband on a particularly cold day. The sky was bluer than the colors on any painter's palette, and the air was so crisp that our jackets crackled when we moved and our skin felt stiff. Yet the snow was soft and deep, skiing felt like flying, and every trail and slope was worth the adventure. The trails were in such good shape that we skied all afternoon without a break and found ourselves alone on the mountain for our last run.

The light softened and the trees began to glow with the reddish hue called alpenglow. As we skied toward the base of the mountain we slowed down and became silent and reverent. We stopped at a ridge to take in the view, suddenly different with the light fading and no people near. Mountains loomed big and dark on the horizon, and the evergreens that lined the slope looked soft and inviting. We stood in silence, taking in the quiet and the cold, crisp air. It occurred to me that if I didn't ski I would most likely have been inside a building at this time of day, wishing for summer and warm weather. Yet here I was with someone I loved, enjoying the winter and feeling more alive than I ever dreamed possible.

Chapter 6

SKIING SPECIFICS FOR WOMEN

WHY LEARN WITH OTHER WOMEN?

Some women feel more comfortable learning new skills with and from other women. There's a different atmosphere in a group of women than in a mixed group. In coed groups girls and women tend to be quieter and question less. There may be an attitude of "keep up with the guys" even if the women are better skiers. In a group of women, it can be easier to ask questions and focus on learning, so you progress more quickly.

Most ski resorts are offering special programs for women, ranging from daily offerings to weekly series to three- or five-day vacation packages. The packages typically include such amenities as lunches, teas, après-ski parties, lectures, equipment seminars, and special sales of gear. The women who coach these events are dedicated to helping women stay in the sport.

Dee Byrne, past PSIA National Demonstration Team member, was skeptical when Carol

"Having coached many events and workshops for women only, I'm amazed to see the support and camaraderie that women can provide in a group. It stays just as competitive, and just as intense, yet the competition is within individuals."

—Dee Byrne, ski school manager

Levine asked her to help build a series of national events for women ski instructors who teach women's programs. "I was curious about the 'women only' thing at first. I thought it bordered on prejudice. I couldn't imagine why any woman would opt out of 'keeping up with the guys.' I'd always done it, and it seemed necessary to gain respect as a skier. Now, having coached many events and workshops for women only, I'm amazed to see the support and camaraderie that women can provide in a group. It stays just as competitive, and just as intense, yet the competition is within individuals, and the intensity goes toward pushing each other as far as possible without sacrificing self-worth by comparing one's own goals or progress with those of others."

Though clinics for women are gaining momentum, many of the offerings are for advanced beginners or intermediates and up. If you're heading to a resort or planning on a learning vacation, call ahead. (See chapter 9 for lists of resorts.)

> "**T**he wonderful thing about skiing is that good technique and strong fundamentals will allow style and freedom of movement without requiring undue levels of strength."
>
> —Carol Levine, training consultant

The author showing proper alignment through a turn.

HOW PHYSICAL DIFFERENCES AFFECT SKIING

Some physical attributes do affect the way women learn to ski. Women who have been skiing for many years, like Vail's Carol Levine, have always known there was something going on. "Women would come to me complaining that they couldn't physically do what their male counterparts could do, despite similar physical fitness and expertise in technique," says Carol. Frustration from her own experiences led her to explore. She began by hosting national seminars and symposiums featuring presentations and research by experts in anatomy, physiology, sociology, and psychology.

"The wonderful thing about skiing," Carol says, "is that good technique and strong fundamentals will allow style and freedom of movement without requiring undue strength." She acknowledges that strength is by far the largest gender difference affecting skiing performance. "Greater muscle mass allows men to go faster and survive technical mistakes. We just have to be more accurate to make up for it."

Accurate movements are a big issue. For a skier to have full control over the skis, the connections between ski, foot, and hip must be effective. If a part of the body is not lined up properly it will affect how the ski moves through the snow. Here is a list of physical gender differences and their possible consequences.

Women tend to have a lower center of mass than men.

- Women tend to have a **lower center of mass.** Center of mass is the place in your body where the most weight is concentrated, found by dividing your body into four equal segments by weight. Your center of mass changes if you wear heavy shoes, carry something in one hand, and so on. Skis and boots alone have quite an influence. A woman's center is lower because of the general "pear shape" of the typical female body. Men usually have wider shoulders and carry more weight above the waist. The difference in strength exacerbates this difference. A lower center of mass tends to distribute weight behind center, causing less control of the tips of the skis and more reliance on the tails. This makes for less effective turns, especially in more difficult snow conditions or steeper slopes. (See the section on heel lifts on pages 87–89.)

- The average woman has a **wider pelvis,** which puts the upper leg bone (femur) at a greater angle to the vertical. This angle is called the Q angle. The amount of tilt varies with individuals; women with a pronounced Q angle may look knock-kneed. This affects the ability to roll the ski on and off its edge and to use skis simultaneously rather than one at a time. Many women with

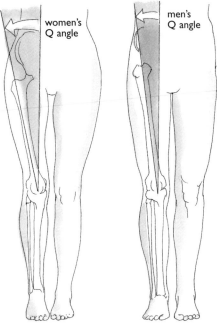

Right: Q angle for men and women. **Below:** Women often use their hips too much at the beginning of a turn, thereby losing the outside edge.

this trait complain that one ski feels as if it's "in the way."

It's important to recognize excessive Q angle because it may increase strain on the knees. Knees are meant to bend forward, not toward each other. Women with this problem can get corrective alignment in their boots and bindings. (See the following section on equipment modifications.)

- Women have **greater mobility in the hip socket** than men. Greater flexibility requires more strength to control and stabilize the body. Women often use their hips too much at the start of a turn, which contributes to loss of control at the end. The body turns up the hill, the uphill shoulder dips, and they lose control of the edge. Fortunately, awareness, fitness, and a good coach can remedy this problem.

EQUIPMENT MODIFICATIONS

Equipment can be customized to help you deal both with fit problems and with the typical differences described above. The main concern is to find a boot fitter or shop that will work with you until you are comfortable and your performance improves. Keep going back until you have it right. Just because you spent a lot of money on equipment or rentals and still have problems, don't assume that you weren't made for this sport or that gear should be perfect right out of the box. Even those of us who have bought new equipment all our lives recognize that we must spend time and energy (and sometimes dollars) to get it to work correctly with our own body peculiarities.

There are many options when a skier's equipment needs adjustment because of body alignment or special comfort or efficiency needs. As customizing gets more sophisticated and easier to do, more "alignment centers" are appearing, and more ski shops are offering special boot-fitting and alignment services. If you're having a painful or frustrating experience, before giving up seek the professional services of a reputable shop and a good ski teacher.

A good ski shop professional begins with the boots. Once the fit is verified, your feet should be checked to see what kind of support you'll need. Most skiers are fine with supportive molded inserts called *footbeds*, but some will need a special orthotic prescribed by a podiatrist or podorthist (see page 100). Support for your feet will allow your boots, and ultimately the skis, to react to movements of your feet.

Many women have restricted forward flexibility in the ankles in addition to a lower center of mass. This can cause balance to be behind center and make the skier "ride the tails." When purchasing or renting boots, be sure you can easily flex your ankle; if you can't do it inside where it's warm, the problem will be worse outside. (See below and pages 98–100.)

Heel lifts

Heel lifts are wedges that are placed inside the boot liner between footbed and liner to improve fit (raising the foot inside the boot for comfort) or fore/aft balancing. They can add leverage against the front of the boot and help bring the skier forward.

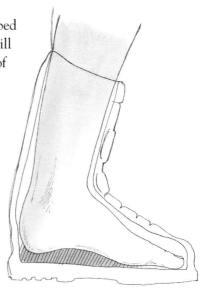

Your foot must be supported properly so you can control the movements of the ski. The shaded area must be filled and contoured to support the foot.

To determine whether you're a candidate for heel lifts, try this: in stocking feet, kneel on a straight chair with your feet hanging naturally behind you. Have a friend place a long carpenter's level against the ball of your foot and adjust it so it is perpendicular, with one end resting on the floor. If there is space between the level and your heel, that space probably should be filled with a heel lift. This is an approximate measurement, but it will give you an idea of how much space is there.

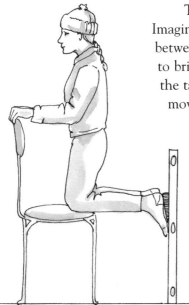

To balance while skiing, you must be able to use your whole foot. Imagine trying to control your skis on your tiptoes! If you don't fill the space between your toe and heel, either you'll be turning on your toes or you'll try to bring the rest of your foot into action by moving your weight aft, over the tails of the skis. Filling the space allows you to remain in balance and move effectively to turn the skis.

When trying heel lifts, experiment with lifts of different thickness. Too much lift can cause the skier to feel stuck on the tails. Heel lifts come in different sizes. If the lift you buy is too wide for your boot, place it under your footbed and trace a line so you can cut it down. You should stand naturally and comfortably in your boots and feel your whole foot, including your heel. You'll know you have too much lift if you feel as though your weight is too far back or your hips are thrust forward.

Checking to see if you're a candidate for heel lifts. Remember this is not an exact measurement: only your performance on the hill will show for sure.

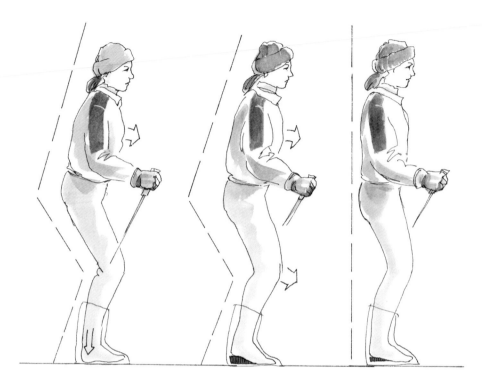

Getting the right amount of heel lift is difficult and requires experimentation since the symptoms of too little lift and too much lift are similar.

Next the professional will check boot cuff alignment. The lower leg may rise toward the knee at an angle, which should be matched by the cuff of the boot so that when you move your leg laterally the boot and the ski react. If your legs are very thin and there is space between the liner and the boot, be sure to fill in this space. Shops usually carry material, similar to neoprene yet stiffer, that can be inserted between boot liner and shell to take up extra room. This should not cause pain; it will make your boot and ski react when you move your leg.

Another way to help with fore/aft balancing is to move the bindings ahead one to two centimeters on the ski. Though sometimes suggested as a blanket cure for all women, this is not always necessary or advisable. Shaped skis in particular may not require the adjustment, and skis meant for women may have this difference built in, but for some women binding placement can radically alter their ability to control the skis.

Finally, the flex of the ankle is checked to see whether the knee flexes over the toes or to the inside or outside of center. Women with a pronounced Q angle may notice their knees flexing into each other rather than forward. Wedges or *cants* are placed under the binding to adjust the angle of the boot on the ski. This is a delicate procedure, and there are many opinions on just how it should be accomplished. Research the credentials of your technician, and be sure you can return to the shop for reworking. So many factors affect alignment that the skier must test the skis' performance on snow to be sure it is correct.

> **"I** can finally feel what you've been describing, and I can do it! . . . I finally understand why people compare skiing to dancing!"
>
> —Kathy, age 46, women's clinic participant

Left: Tera is rippin' it up! **Below:** With a gap between your leg and the boot cuff **(A)**, you'll have difficulty controlling the ski. You can add a filler to help your leg meet the boot **(B)**, so it's easier for you to control the ski.

Left undetected and unaccounted for, physical problems can detract from your adventure. At best you'll feel frustrated, at worst they can cause injury. Hire a good coach to check you out early in your skiing career, and get your equipment modified if necessary. As you progress, pay attention to what you feel. Skiing is a sport of sensations, and if those you feel are not comfortable or are not allowing you to ski the runs you'd like with the control and finesse you want, explore the options above. You'll be amazed at how your experience will improve. "I feel so much more relaxed! I can finally feel what you've been describing, and I can do it!" Kathy, a three-year skiing veteran, was ecstatic after placing heel lifts in her boots. "I feel so much more fluid and rhythmical! I finally understand why people compare skiing to dancing! I wish I'd known this sooner."

Chapter 7

BUYING YOUR OWN GEAR

Understanding your skiing personality is of utmost importance if you're going to end up with gear that will last for a while. That profile won't emerge until you're relatively confident about your wants and needs.

After your first skiing adventure, you'll undoubtedly want to continue. Once you're hooked the next step is to buy your own gear, but you need to know when, where, and how to do so. It's wise to wait until you've skied several times and begun to discover the type of skier you'll be. Understanding your skiing personality is of utmost importance if you're going to end up with gear that will last for a while. That profile won't emerge until you're relatively confident about your wants and needs. Compare it to buying a car. If you know exactly what you want, the process may be trying, but you usually get favorable results. But if you wander into a showroom uninitiated and unaware, you may leave with a car that you later discover doesn't fit you as well as you expected. The same is true for ski gear.

Consider waiting to buy gear until your learning curve reaches a plateau and you know how often you'll ski. Most of the new technology in skis allows for a broad range of skiing ability and supports a fairly steep growth curve, yet it's still prudent to wait until at least your third outing.

Once you've established your skiing patterns—how often you will ski and where—you can begin to look for a retail shop that will get to know your needs and provide customized service. Walk around the store and see how engaging and attentive the sales staff is. This will give you a clue to how you'll be treated. Check return policies. The last thing you need is to make a mistake on a big-ticket item only to find out that the seller won't help you correct it.

Once the store passes the "service" screen, look to see what products are carried and how much variety there is. Investigate whether there are versions appropriate for women. Many smaller shops don't carry a wide enough size range to meet the needs of smaller or larger people, especially women. Before you make a purchase, be sure you fit in with the shop and its staff.

The options for purchase can be overwhelming.

Finally, get your coach to help if possible. Someone who has seen your potential and is aware of what's in the marketplace can answer questions and help you avoid the typical pitfalls of first-time buyers.

SHOPPING FOR CLOTHES

Shopping for clothes may sound like a fun day at the mall, but if you're going to stay with the sport it's essential to invest in good technical gear that will keep you warm, dry, comfortable, and of course stylish. Check out the fall issues of *Ski* and *Skiing* magazines for the latest choices. Each year the retail world comes out with new fabrics, new styles, and useful gadgets. For example, my new parka has a chamois attached inside one of the pockets for cleaning glasses and goggles. Another publication that is great for getting the latest and greatest from the consumer's point of view is *Inside Tracks*, which reviews clothing and equipment as well as resorts and services. (See chapter 9.)

First things first

The most important purchase is the layer next to your skin. A multitude of fabrics are designed to keep warmth in and moisture out, and they come in designs from skintight to looser fitting. You can find ultrafeminine designs that are just as functional as "expedition" underwear. There are also fleece bras and panties to layer under your fleece or polypropylene turtleneck and thermals. It's your choice. Just be sure to pick underwear that is comfortable and easily laundered. It won't do any good at all if you wind up wearing your standard T-shirt because something binds.

PRICE RANGES

• • • • • • • • • • • • • • • • • • • •

You can spend a lot or just enough on clothing and equipment. This is usually dependent on how much you shop around. The lower prices listed below are rock-bottom, so if you get close to these . . . buy two!

Clothing

Expect to pay $30 to $60 each for top and bottom long underwear. Socks will run from $8 to $20. Good-quality gloves or mittens run from $40 to $100, depending on the durability of the materials. Hats start at about $15 in a ski shop, but you can often find stylish hats that work well in department stores for less. Helmets are a bit more expensive: $80 to $150+ for more style or features. Expect to pay $200 to $500 for a stylish parka, and the same again for pants.

(continued next page)

Right: There are a variety of undergarments available. Be sure what you choose is comfortable and warm. **Below and bottom:** Sweaters are a matter of style. That's when shopping is fun!

Your next layer should consist of fleece or a wool-blend sweater on top and fleece pants below. If you choose a one-piece garment, be sure it's made so you can use the toilet. There's nothing more frustrating than being in a hurry and discovering you have to remove four layers to relieve yourself! Again, the possibilities are endless, but try them on over your foundation layer to be sure nothing binds or is uncomfortable. Consider adding a fleece vest for warmer days when long sleeves are unnecessary or to wear over the regular fleece top or sweater if it's especially cold.

Outer layers

The outer layer is what defines "the look" for a skier. Whether you go "technical" like a racer, "new wave" like a mogul skier, "expedition" like the extreme or back country skier, "free ride" like a snowboard generation-Xer, or choose to look as if you've walked out of the ski fashion pages, the choice is yours. You can pick virtually any style and still get the features that will make your investment worth the dollars and time spent. Here's a list of features to think about.

- **Fabrics and materials.** Consider the climate when you decide what type of fabric you'll need. By far the biggest detriment to my own skiing is the cold. Know what you're buying and how it will stack up in cold or wet weather. Most technical gear is now waterproof (impervious to water) and breathable and has a warmth rating. You may be able to get away with water-resistant fabric, but only if you won't be skiing in significant snowstorms or rain. A good parka and pants that are waterproof may be able to double for winter hiking and other activities. Although they're more expensive, waterproof outer layers will ultimately save you money if you don't need additional rain gear.

- **Venting.** If you worry about the cold, you should also worry about overheating and then getting chilled. Many manufacturers now provide armpit zips or vents in parkas that will let out excess heat, then zip shut for warmth.

- **Pockets.** Pockets are a must for carrying "stuff." Be sure they're placed where you can reach them easily and have zipper pulls made for use with gloves or mittens. But if the jacket has too many pockets,

When selecting outer clothing, you can choose between "expedition" clothing **(top)**, "new wave" or "free ride" clothing **(middle)**, and "technical" clothing **(right)**.

PRICE RANGES

(continued from previous page)

Gear

Boots will range from $300 to $600, bindings $75 to $200, and skis $280 to $800. However, most retail stores offer packages designed for different ability levels, and these range in price depending on what is included. The prices range anywhere from $350 to $1,500. Beware the "deals," and be sure to get boots that work for you, even if you must pay extra. Some enterprising shops are even including free mounting (setting up your bindings on your skis) and season-long tuning with the packages for a nominal fee. This is usually worth it, since repair-shop costs add up quickly.

you might forget where you put your keys. Also, side pockets on the hips make you look wider, so if that's an issue, be sure pockets on pants are forward of the hips or in the back. Some pants even have pockets on the legs; be sure the fabric is sturdy enough to handle what you put in them.

- **Fleece lining.** A great option in an outer layer is a zip-out fleece lining. This makes a parka more versatile, since it turns into a windbreaker in the spring. Other options include cozy fleece-lined collars and cuffs.

- **Hoods.** Check to see if there's a hood hiding in the collar of the coat. Hoods are a great option in stormy weather and windproof your head.

- **Parka length.** Shorter parkas provide free action of the legs and show a skier's movements more clearly to those watching. Longer coats are warmer and keep the seat warm on chairlifts. Manufacturers are now putting drawstring waist cords in longer parkas to provide the best of both worlds.

Bib pants provide an extra layer of warmth but can be a challenge in the restroom.

- **Ankle and wrist cuffs.** Be sure the cuffs of both parka and pants are adjustable so you can get them on and off easily and snug them tight.

- **Zippers.** Pants with full-length zippers covered by wind flaps are easy to add or remove as an extra layer. Parkas with removable sleeves also add versatility. Be sure zippers are heavy duty and tabbed.

- **Bib pants and one-piece suits.** Bib pants provide extra warmth since they add an extra layer on top, but they can be hard to remove in rest rooms unless the straps go outside the top layer. One-piece suits are less expensive overall yet are not as versatile as parka and pants combinations. These too are difficult in the rest room. I've dropped many sleeves into the toilet and had to hold them under the hand dryer!

Accessories

There are two basic types of accessories for skiing; those you have to have and those that are nice to have. I've separated the two categories so you can set your priorities. The truly necessary items are:

- **Socks.** Buy the very best (polypropylene or wool, not cotton), and buy more than one pair. Change socks each time you ski, since sweat and dirt can interfere with wicking. On really cold days you'll want to bring a spare pair to change into at lunch. Be sure the socks fit you (they do come in sizes), are knee length, and have no ribs. You can buy good socks at most sporting goods stores, but you're more likely to get the best socks for skiing in a ski shop. I like Smartwool socks for their wicking ability, warmth, and comfort. (See page 29.)

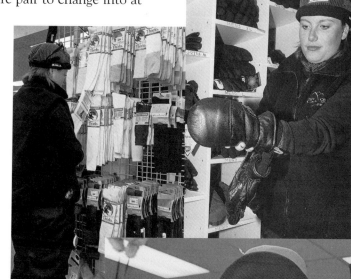

Top left: Karin chooses new socks. **Top right:** Deciding on gloves or mittens. **Above:** Shopping for a hat.

- **Gloves and mittens.** When buying gloves and mittens, again consider the climate. If you'll be in extreme cold, getting them a bit large will let you add a thin polypropylene liner so you can adjust zippers and bindings without having bare hands. Also, consider mittens or gloves with built-in pouches for handwarmer packs. These are a bit more expensive, but they help you enjoy skiing longer. Swany makes the warmest leather gloves I've found, and they also make mittens with a zippered pocket for a heat pouch. When it snows or is wet outside, waterproofing is essential for keeping hands warm and dry. Consider gloves or mittens that have waterproofing built in or that you can apply waterproofing to. Finally, in spring temperatures you'll want a lighter-weight glove. Resist the temptation to go barehanded. A fall on coarse spring snow, or catching the edges of your skis can cause severe cuts.

- **Hats and helmets.** The main object in purchasing a hat is warmth. From there the options are endless. Style changes constantly, and hats can help you

Helmets must fit snugly.

make a statement. If you want a really warm hat, look for one lined with WindStopper fleece, which will protect you well on windy, cold days. Most helmets are warm as well, but some don't cover the ears and leave a gap at the back of the neck. If this is true of the one you choose, look for a balaclava—a thin head and neck covering made to fit under a helmet. Be sure the helmet doesn't slide around on your head as you move, that you can hear well, and that your peripheral vision isn't impaired.

- **Neck gaiters.** Although not always necessary, when cold or snowy weather hits this accessory is a must. Neck gaiters fill in the space between your goggles and your collar. The most comfortable ones are simple tubes made of cozy fleece and slide on over your head. There are also more fashionable ones made of fabrics designed to coordinate with outerwear and lined with fleece. These are usually like triangular face masks, with Velcro tabs that fasten behind the head. They make cold-weather skiing a bit more stylish and feminine.

Velcro

microfleece inside

pretty print outside

This is a neck gaiter you can make yourself!

- **Eyewear.** Goggles are a must for protecting the eyes from wind, sun, and precipitation. Generally an amber lens is the most versatile and is particularly good in cloudy weather or flat light. Some people like rose lenses, but I haven't found one that brings out the definition in the slope as well as the amber. Dark lenses will make your eyes more comfortable on brighter days. Whatever lens you choose, be sure it screens out ultraviolet rays. If you wear glasses, there are goggles made especially to go over them and not fog up. You can buy a no-fog cloth and a Skigee, which is a kind of windshield wiper for your goggles. Both these items are relatively inexpensive ($3 to $5) and lengthen the life of your lenses by preventing scratches. Sunglasses are more comfortable on sunny days. Be sure to bring the goggles along just in case. When purchasing glasses, look for wraparound styles that will block wind and permit peripheral vision. A strap will keep you from losing them when you go inside. Eye protection is a must for skiing. If you can't see well, you won't be comfortable. Don't scrimp on your eyes.

Items that are nice to have but not essential include

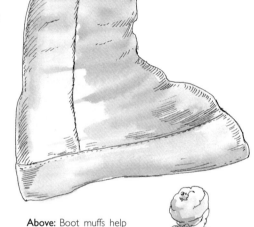

- **Boot heaters.** If you worry about keeping your feet warm, you can get boot heaters. For about $150, you can buy battery-operated pads that fasten to your footbed inside the boot. There are switches on your boots, so you can turn them on and off and regulate the heat. They must be installed by the ski shop, but they're worth the money if you're prone to cold feet. A cheaper option, at about $40, is a neoprene sleeve that fits over your ski boot, but these boot warmers can be frustrating if you need to adjust the buckles.

Above: Boot muffs help keep out moisture and keep in warmth.

- **Heat packets for feet and hands.** These warmers sell for about $2 a pair. There are packets for hands and toes. Once activated by shaking or squeezing, they last up to seven hours. You can also buy them by the box if you have a family or will ski often in cold weather.

- **Fanny warmers.** This waterproof cover, usually made of neoprene or similar material, is worn over your outerwear to protect your seat on cold or wet chairlifts. Expect to pay about $40.

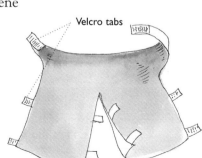

Velcro tabs

Right: Fanny warmers help keep your buttocks dry, making for more time on the slopes.

- **Nose warmers.** As I was riding the chairlift with Sylvie Richard, a ski professional at Mount Snow, Vermont, I noticed she had a fleece cone over her nose and attached to her goggles. She said a friend had made it. I thought it was a fabulous idea! It protects the nose from frostbite without fogging up your goggles and feels very cozy next to your face.

A nose warmer provides protection against frostbite.

- **Neck pockets.** In spring, when you tend to shed layers, a zippered pouch that hangs around your neck can hold valuables such as cash, lift pass, credit card, and room key so you won't risk leaving them in the pocket of a parka stored in the base lodge or tossed in a pile on the ground.

> "I thought it would be so much easier if I had my own boots. . . . I thought I knew what I was doing, but I felt like I do when I go to get my car fixed."
>
> —Kim, age 40, nurse practitioner

SHOPPING FOR SKI EQUIPMENT

Purchasing your own ski equipment can be overwhelming. Be prepared for shop technicians to ask you lots of questions. (If they don't, go somewhere else.) A good salesperson will ask about your ability level, how long you've been skiing, how often you ski, what type of terrain you like, how fit you are, what equipment you are currently using, and what you hope to accomplish after you purchase your gear.

Your first purchase: Boots

Boots are the most important purchase you will make, whether you are a novice or seasoned pro. Boots can make skiing next to flying or create almost insurmountable obstacles to progress.

Kim bought new boots fairly early on in her skiing career. She still remembers the pain: "I thought it would be so much easier if I had my own boots. I went to the first ski shop I could find. I thought I knew what I was doing, but I felt like I do when I go to get my car fixed. The salesperson referred to features and used terms that I didn't know about, and because I felt intimidated, I went along with whatever was recommended.

"I sat on the bench to be fitted and asked for a specific pair of boots just like when I buy shoes. The salesperson patiently explained that those boots didn't come in my size and wouldn't be appropriate for me anyway, then went on to sell me boots that caused pain in my ankles until I ditched them and bought new ones. The problem was that I wasn't yet confident that I knew what I wanted, and I hadn't done my homework. Even so, that shop lost my business." (See pages 31–32 on types of boot entry.)

Read the articles in the fall issues of skiing magazines. They always review the new equipment and give information about what may be right for you. Then consult a coach or shop employee you trust. Ask questions and find out whether the shop will stand by the sale and help you with retrofit. Even good boots may end up being painful after a few outings, and it's important to be able to go back to the shop where you bought them and ask for help with fitting. Many people continue to ski with pain in their feet or even give up the sport because they fail to go back and ask for help. Many shops even build in a service plan for their boots. This way you can be sure you get what you invest in—a pain-free day on the slopes.

The author fits her daughter Karin for new boots.

Jan couldn't believe how long she spent in the ski shop getting her boots fitted. "I had this sharp pain by my ankle, and it just wouldn't quit. I knew that the next size up was too big, so I knew I needed to work with the pain. It didn't start as soon as I put the boot on; it would start after I flexed my ankles a few times. The shop technician did some work to the inner boot, and I had to go skiing to see if it worked. It took three trips, but now my feet are really happy!"

Properly fitted boots may feel a bit tight at first. As you walk around in them and get moving, the discomfort will lessen. Ski boots are designed to give support and are much stiffer than other athletic footwear. You shouldn't be able to slide your fingers down the front or rear of the boot when it is buckled. It may take some time to adjust to the rigidity, but you should still be able to flex your ankle forward with a significant range of movement. When you do this, the boot should move with your leg. Look for a boot that fits snugly around your calf with your heel and ankle seated firmly into the liner. If the boot is difficult to flex forward, look at the height. If it goes too far up your leg, look for a shorter cuff. There are more and more "women's" boots—which tend to have a lower cuff and softer flex—on the market, although most boots are unisex. If the boots fit well, it doesn't really matter whether they're unisex or not. Again, ask your boot fitter or coach for assistance.

Jane, a client in a women's seminar, assumed she would always be a so-so skier. The seminar included a presentation on boot fitting, and Jane asked the clinician to check her boots. Sure enough, there was a wide gap between Jane's leg and the boot. When she moved her leg, the boot wouldn't respond directly. Jane had the fit of the boot adjusted and immediately felt the difference. "I now believe I can learn to ski better, and it's all due to that simple adjustment of my boots." Ultimately, the boot is the connection between you and your ski, and pain or extra room inside will take away from your comfort and your ability to control the ski. If it hurts, or if you don't think your performance is up to snuff, ask for help.

In summary, look for your boot fitter first. Then find a boot that has the right cuff width and height for your leg. Be sure you can flex the boot easily and that there are adjustments you can make to soften or stiffen the cuff. Usually, high-cost boots are too stiff and the shaft too high for most women. However, if you're a small, lightweight woman, consider high-end junior boots, which are often as sophisticated as adult boots yet provide a better fit. Finally, make sure the boots fit and that your boot fitter can help you with any ongoing problems (see pages 86–89). Ultimately—go with what fits your foot (and leg) the best.

Footbeds

Perhaps the best additional investment when you buy boots is the footbed, an insert molded to your foot and placed inside the boot. The footbed supports your foot as you balance and work the ski, transmitting movement more seamlessly from your foot to the boot to the ski. For those with particularly "difficult" feet, an orthotic that is prescribed and molded by a licensed podorthist may be more appropriate. Again, your boot fitter is the key to your success. (See also pages 32 and 86–89.)

The footbed is an integral part of the ski boot for most people. The footbed fits the shape of your foot, cupping the heel to decrease movement. It also supports your arch.

Buying your own skis

Like boots, new skis are rated each year in skiing magazines (see chapter 9). The clearest message for purchasing skis is to try before you buy. The easiest way to try out skis is to attend a "demo day" at a resort. These events usually occur early in the season, and you usually pay one fee to try out several kinds of skis and boots. The down side is that many other folks will be there too, for the same reason, and you often can't get the length or size you need. The long lines you encounter are also likely to be discouraging. However, you may be able to ski with a salesperson or ski professional who can guide you toward the right ski for you and then coach you to discover the performance capabilities of the skis. Think of it as technical assistance for a new computer. Your pro will help you dial into the ski through adjusting your technique. This tactic is so successful that many resorts are now offering this service right out of their retail shops and putting the cost of the demo toward the price of the skis, should you choose to buy. That is one "deal" that's worth it! If you can't ski with a pro during your demo, the shop salesperson can help you narrow your choices to two or three. Here are some things to consider.

First, the demonstration bindings will add weight and bulk to the skis. This can affect performance, and the ski will perform differently when mounted with your own binding. Small, light women are most affected by this. Second, be sure the demo skis are tuned properly. If they've been used repeatedly, the tuning may not be good, making your trial ineffective.

Demo skis in the length you will buy. If you're forced to try longer ones you won't get a true indication of how they'll perform, since many modern skis work very differently with even a small difference in length. (See pages 33–34.)

Next, be sure to try all the demo skis on the same terrain. Pick trails that will allow you to change your speed and your turn shape and adjust to flatter and steeper pitches. Be sure to ski a variety of conditions including moguls (assuming you're ready for them). If the skis are meant for particular conditions like powder or bumps, ski on what they were designed for.

Finally, pay careful attention to how the skis react. Are they easy to turn? Do you feel stable at speed? Can you hold the edge? Your boots create a system with your ski, and if the boot is inappropriate for the type of ski, the result will be less than favorable. Ask about the compatibility of your boots with the skis you choose.

What about skis designed for women?

Manufacturers used to put an L on a shorter length of the regular ski or take out some of the inner materials of the design and call it a "women's ski." Now, however, they are paying particular attention to women and recognizing that women are as varied as men and deserve better than to find the same model of ski with different colors on top. Now the options abound, which can be overwhelming when choosing a new ski.

In general, women's skis are softer flexing, come in shorter lengths, are lighter in construction, and are designed to have the bindings mounted farther forward or have a larger "sweet spot"—turning zone, like the sweet spot on a tennis raquet. When you're deciding what skis to try, ask how the construction of women's models differs from the regular line.

Choosing length and ski category

Determining what length to try is perhaps the most significant issue you will face. While some skis are best at certain lengths, there's usually a length you shouldn't exceed. With the development of ski design, manufacturers have learned to make skis that perform extremely well in shorter lengths, so it's no longer necessary to use a longer ski for stability or security at speed or in differing conditions. Today's skis are more versatile, lighter, and shorter than ever. Resist the urge to buy beyond your comfort length thinking you'll grow into it. With the exception of learning on extremely short skis (GLM; see pages 33–34), the skis you're using by your second or third week will most likely be a good length. Again, ask your ski professional if you're not sure.

I've skied all my life and have seen skiing sages move from recommending longer and longer skis in the 1960s, to really short skis in the 1970s, back to longer skis in the 1980s and early 1990s, then to the shorter, shaped skis of the late 1990s. My skiing skill has changed with this evolution. When the recommended lengths were longer, I skied worse. As the recommendations moved to short, I could suddenly ski again! As an accomplished skier five feet, five inches tall, weighing 120 pounds, I use 170-centimeter skis and love them. Even my racing skis are only 173 centimeters long. Don't be fooled by shop technicians or ski pros who recommend longer skis. Do some research of your own first.

The typical categories to choose from are race, high performance, sport, and recreational skis, but with the advances in ski design these lines are blurring. Owing to improved geometry and lightweight construction materials, a ski that will perform well for an expert skier is often forgiving enough for a woman who is less skilled. So you are probably better off buying a sport or high performance ski as long as you purchase the right length. Again, try before you buy. And if there's an option to take a lesson on the demo skis, do it. You'll get more from your purchase if you have more information.

Ask the shop technician to explain binding characteristics.

Bindings

Bindings hold your feet to the skis. Because of new research and safety requirements, manufacturers are building bindings that are safer and more effective. You'll need to consider binding weight and range of DIN setting, which determines the point where the binding releases. Your weight, height, age, and skiing ability contribute to your DIN setting. If your number is 6, you'll want to purchase a binding with a range from 5 to 12. Your personal setting should fall close to the middle of the range. If it's at the low end, you probably bought more binding than you need (which costs more money). If it's at the upper end, the binding probably isn't sturdy enough.

Another consideration for bindings is their weight. In general, the lighter the better. Manufacturers of bindings are now using lightweight materials such as titanium alloys that are beefy and safe, yet don't add a lot of weight to your ski. Lighter materials are higher in price (they can add up to $100), but this is usually well worth it, since skis are much more maneuverable when they're lighter.

Some bindings have a riser built in or are connected from toe to heel. The riser gives more leverage and generally makes the ski easier to turn, and the connected bindings allow the ski to flex more naturally. Both of these options work well, but the binding must form a system with the boot and ski. Ask your shop technician and your coach for advice.

Poles

Poles have become lighter and easier to manage. The most important consideration is length. Turn the pole over and grip it beneath the basket. As you grasp the pole, your forearm should be parallel with the floor. If you do buy poles that are too long, you can usually get them cut down to fit.

Be sure the grip is the right size for you. If it's too large your hand will tire; if it's too small your hand will continually slip down the pole when the basket hits the snow. Check that the strap is easy to enter and exit and that it will let you swing the pole freely. Plastic grips with no straps restrict pole swing.

The basket must also be the right size. If it's too small the pole will stick too far into soft snow; if it's too large it adds unnecessary weight. Grasp the pole and swing it to feel the weight. It should feel light and free.

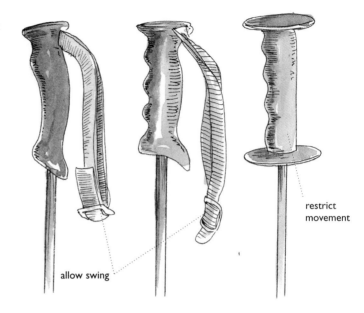

restrict movement

allow swing

Straps are preferable to pole-grips to aid in pole-swing.

Buying gear for your kids

Probably the biggest thing you can do to ensure your child's success on the slopes is to provide proper equipment. There are many good products on the market, yet it takes care to get the right fit and function.

The factors determining the proper ski length are age, ability, strength, and weight. Here are some general guidelines: For tots, the skis should be about chest height. For five- to seven-year-old beginners, chin height works, and when they become intermediates the ski should be about eye height. For seven- to twelve-year-old beginners, start with eye height and go to head height for intermediates. For advanced skiers the length should be at the discretion of the coach, who will understand your child's skiing needs. Skis that are too long will be difficult to maneuver. If skis are too short, your child may turn the skis too sharply, impairing control and stability.

Most companies are now making shaped skis for kids, which can help a young child learn turning skills more easily. More advanced kids get the benefit of really shaping turns at slower speeds. If you choose a shaped ski for your child, whether renting or purchasing, get them shorter; the ski should be about chin height. Be sure the ski isn't too stiff longitudinally, so it will bend under the weight and help your child control the arc of the turn. If not, the ski will take more energy to turn.

The way boots fit is crucial. To get an approximate size, place the child's stocking foot on the bottom of the plastic outer shell, then remove the inner boot liner and place the foot inside it. If the fit is all right, have the child put on the whole boot and run

When children have the right equipment, they always have more fun!

When your child is gliding easily down the slopes . . . you'll be glad you spent your time and energy wisely.

around. Be sure there is toe wiggle room and that the child is comfortable. A boot that fits is more likely to be warm. Ski boots are not going to be as comfortable as sneakers, however, and the boots must not be too big. When they are, the child sacrifices control of the foot and consequently the ski, causing frustration and a poor learning experience for beginners and seasoned skiers alike. Give the child plenty of time to get used to the tighter fit. It's far better to go for current fit and trade the boots in when the child outgrows them than to allow for growing room.

Another concern when buying ski boots is whether to buy rear-entry or mid- to front-entry boots (see page 32). The determining factors should be the fit, whether the child can operate the buckle system independently, and whether the boots will bend at the ankle. Being able to bend or "flex" the boots is central to performance and comfort; if you can't flex the boots easily with your hands in the warm ski shop, chances are your child won't be able to do it while wearing them outside.

The best skis and boots in the world are of little consequence if the bindings don't provide a safe release system. Your child's height, weight, and ability determine the proper binding and binding release setting. It is imperative that the binding you buy releases when it's supposed to and holds the foot secure otherwise. Once the proper release setting has been determined (see the section on bindings above), check that the bindings you purchase are designed for your child's size and ability. Resist the temptation to buy a cheaper binding designed for small children or a binding your child can "grow into" but that is too much for the current size. Last, look for easy operation. Some bindings are difficult for children to get into and out of by themselves, so an adult has to be on hand to help.

Finally, decide whether your child needs poles. Most three- and four-year-olds don't, and poles can detract from their ability to control their feet. Most ski programs start even older children without them, since poles often are a safety hazard as kids learn to balance on their skis. Once the child is managing green to blue runs easily, the poles should be introduced as a help for balance and propelling across flat terrain.

To determine pole fit, turn the pole upside down and place the grip on the ground near the child's foot. When the child grasps the pole just beneath the basket, the elbow should form a 90-degree angle, and the forearm should be parallel to the ground. Don't buy poles to grow into; this will create poor arm carriage and difficulty in balancing. Poles that are too short will also interfere with balance and won't be effective in propelling across flats.

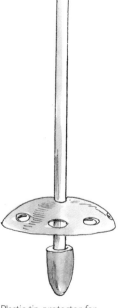

Plastic tip protector for child's pole.

Whether you buy poles with straps or plastic grips, be sure the child's mittens or gloves fit into them. Straps are useful in falls, since they keep the poles with the child, and they allow for a better pole swing than plastic grips, but for smaller children the grips can be easier to maneuver. Lightweight poles with protective points are a definite plus for the smaller set.

Shopping for proper equipment is time consuming and often confusing, but it will pay off in the long run. When your child is gliding easily down the slopes surrounded by the smiles and giggles of the whole class, you'll be glad you spent your time and energy wisely.

EASING THE FINANCIAL PAIN

If retail shopping is making you feel a bit nauseous thinking about all the macaroni-and-cheese dinners you'll have to eat to make up for all the dollars spent on gear, take an antacid and read on. You have some options. "I thought my dad was going to flip out!" recalls Jan. "The day we bought my first pair of 'real' ski boots, he looked sort of green when he handed over the credit card. We had always shopped at the ski swap before. I remember that there was even new stuff there. You could really make out great!"

End-of-season sales

The best option for purchasing great stuff at cheaper prices begins mid to late February, which is sale season for ski shops. Retailers begin to order inventory for the next season in February, trying to empty their shops as summer approaches. As a result, you can often get great gear at a bargain price if you're willing to wait until late winter to use it. Prices can drop 10 to 50 percent. This is really perfect timing for new skiers, since they will often have skied enough by February to know what they want. The only danger is that whatever you need could be sold out. This is time for serious shopping!

Ski swap savvy

If purchasing your gear and clothing from a retail shop seems too pricey, consider attending a ski swap. Typically held in the fall, these events are usually sponsored by ski clubs or schools and feature gear from folks who are upgrading and bring in last year's castoffs on consignment. In recent years, ski shops have been getting into the act, bringing their close-outs and older merchandise they want to unload. Prices are usually very reasonable, though more expensive than for the used equipment. You have to get there early for the best variety and pricing. Buyer beware, however, since these items don't come with any shop guarantee. Some of these events are being staffed with shop technicians, boot fitters, coaches, and instructors so you can at least get advice.

Lease programs for kids' gear

Another option for saving major cash outlay is to lease your children's gear directly from the retail shop. These folks know kids grow faster than they will wear out the gear—so much faster that retailers can lease the same gear (or sell it used) and still get value. Sign up for the program when you pay retail for the first set of gear. During the year, if your child grows you can change equipment at no cost. At the end of the year, you turn in the gear and pay a small fee to upgrade for the next year. Other lease programs involve a membership fee (usually the price of a middle-of-the-road package, $100 and up depending on the child's age and ability) but no upgrade fee. Programs vary, but they usually save money for parents, especially if your child will be skiing often.

MAINTAINING YOUR GEAR

Once you've purchased your gear, you need to know how to care for it. Just like your car, your ski equipment needs maintenance and proper storage. And just like your car, it will work only as well as it is maintained.

Tune it up

Tuning keeps your skis performing as they were designed to do. Every five to seven times you ski, your skis need attention. This number increases if you're skiing hard snow, and it can decrease a bit in softer conditions. Skiing on skis that need tuning is like driving a car with a shaky transmission. They accelerate and decelerate unpredictably, and you feel less and less confident that you'll get where you're going in one piece.

There are two ways to tune your gear: do it yourself or hire a shop technician. If you choose to pay someone to tune your skis (and this is often the most convenient method) it's like taking your car to a garage. Do a bit of research first so you understand what you need and can be sure you get what you pay for. Expect to pay $15 to $50, depending on the services you require. To tune your own skis, you need the right tools and the right tactics.

Tuning is relatively straightforward, yet a mystique has built up around it owing to new technologies and the wide array of tools available for the job. (For information on purchasing tools, see chapter 9.) Basically, the goal of tuning is to make the base of the ski flat and flush with the metal edge and to create a smooth, sharp edge that has a uniform geometry (bevel). The sidebar on the next pages explains the steps involved, but until you can have an experienced person demonstrate so you feel confident that you won't damage your skis, it may be best to leave it to a professional. After reading

A good, clean angle of edge to base provides good edge grip and smooth gliding through the snow.

Once you've purchased your gear, you need to know how to care for it. Just like your car, your ski equipment needs maintenance and proper storage. And just like your car, it will work only as well as it is maintained.

TUNING

• •

First, fasten the ski brake flush with the bottom of the ski. This can be done with heavy-duty rubber bands, or you can buy a special fastener in a ski shop. Next, place the ski in a tabletop vise attached to your tuning bench. You can purchase a portable tuning bench from Reliable Racing, but the workbench in your garage works, too.

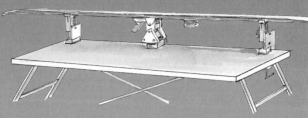

A garage workbench can work for tuning your skis, but benches designed just for tuning skis will keep your frustration level lower.

Prepare your bases by cleaning them with household solvent, since dirt and grime build up on the bases just as they do on the bottoms of your shoes. You can buy environmentally friendly solvent from your ski shop.

Start by checking to see if the base is level. If it's higher than the edges (convex), you must scrape it with a steel scraper. If the base is concave, or lower than the edges, file the edges with a flat file. Either of these tasks can be completed with a tool built for the job made by SkiVisions called the Base Flattener. If your bases are in extremely bad shape, it's worth the cash to take them to the local shop and get them ground by a machine, which takes far less time and effort.

Check your base for significant gouges. Hitting rocks or other debris on the mountain can take its toll. If you find a gouge, it will need to be filled with base material (P-Tex). This is best done by a shop unless you are an expert or can get one to show you. P-Tex comes in candles like wax; it's heated and melted into the ski, then the base is flattened again so there is no irregularity where the new material is. This needs to be done before you store your skis for long periods, since these gouges house moisture and can cause the base to separate from the edge with repeated heating and cooling.

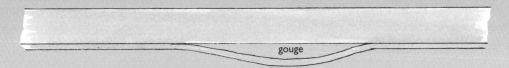

Gouges should be repaired as soon as possible since they can cause the ski to separate from the edge.

Once the base is flat, it's time to make the edges sharp. First, deburr them with a stone. You can feel burrs on the edges if you run your finger lightly along the metal. These rough spots can create drag on the ski. Use a diamond stone to remove the "big chunks" before attending to the edge geometry. Stones come in different meshes for different degrees of roughness. These are also handy to carry in your pocket in case of mishap.

When skis had less sidecut, it was common to file the edges square to the ski with a simple flat file. Now, with shaped skis, if the edges are too square, owing to the wider tip and constant edge contact with the snow, they will "hook up" with even the slightest pressure and throw the skier forward. To combat this, the ski's edges are beveled; the base edge so that the ski can be rolled into a turn, and the side edge so that it grips the snow.

(continued next page)

TUNING

• •

(continued from previous page)

The most common edge
geometry for shaped skis is a one-degree side
bevel and a one-degree base bevel. A variety of handheld devices
for this purpose can be ordered from Reliable Racing Supply (see chapter 9). These
gadgets contain small files housed in plastic casings to hold them at the precise angles
needed. They are also designed to do the job with more finesse and less
elbow grease.

Top: The diamond stone is a great tool to carry in your pocket. **Above:** Tools for edge-filing.

Once the edges are shaped and sharp, they can be polished with a
Gummi stone. This tool is the same shape as the diamond stone but feels
soft and gummy, hence the name. This last step will make the edges smooth
(fast) and will remove any filings from the edges and help prepare the skis for waxing. Wipe the whole
length of both skis with a rag, then wax them as explained in the text.

A tuning kit consists of the following basics:

- rags
- metal and plastic scrapers
- edging tools
- Scotch-Brite pads
- waxing iron

- tabletop vise
- assorted files
- diamond stone
- brass-bristle brush
- wax

- straightedge
- base-flattening tools
- Gummi stone
- nylon-bristle brush
- solvent

Of course you can purchase complete tuning kits as well. These range in price from very basic at
about $50 to very complete, including folding table, for as much as $500.

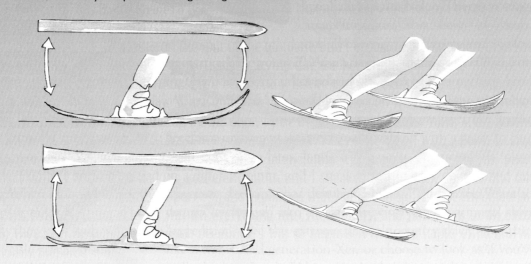

When a traditional ski **(top)** is bent into a reverse camber in a turn, the tip and tail are not in contact with the snow.
Because of their sidecut, shaped skis **(above)** maintain edge control with the snow all along the length of the ski.

about how to tune your skis, you're properly armed to go to a shop and pay someone else to do it. Be sure to ask about their procedures, and be sure you get all the steps you pay for. If the shop asks if you want to "detune" tip and tail, the answer is probably "no" if you have a shaped ski. These skis are built shorter and are designed to use the whole edge, whereas traditional skis had a certain amount of edge at tip and tail that was not in contact with the snow. If your shaped ski reacts unpredictably, try detuning it.

Waxing

After the skis are tuned, it's time to wax them. The ski shop will do this as part of the job, but you should be able to do it yourself between tunings. Many skiers think waxing is just for going fast. Not so. Waxing is important for maintaining the health of your bases. The base material of your skis is porous and can trap moisture and dirt from the snow surface. Coating the bases with wax protects the skis from foreign substances, not to mention keeping them gliding and sliding efficiently.

Waxing should be done every weekend if you're a weekend skier and every two or three days if you're skiing daily. The best way is hot waxing; you buy blocks of wax and melt it along the ski, then spread it evenly over the base, keeping the iron moving. Don't use more wax than the ski will absorb, since you'll just have to scrape it off.

1.   Deep clean the base with a brass-bristle brush, which can be purchased from a ski shop or ordered by mail from Reliable Racing Supply.

2.   Melt the wax onto the skis with an iron. You can purchase a special iron or buy an old flatiron at a garage sale; using your regular one makes your shirts come out funny. The iron should be on the lowest setting; if it smokes, it's too hot. Melt the wax against the tip of the iron and let it drip along the ski, then spread it evenly over the base, keeping the iron moving. Don't use more wax than the ski will absorb, since you'll just have to scrape it off.

3.   Once the wax cools to room temperature, scrape off the excess with a metal or plastic scraper (an old credit card will work).

4.   Use a nylon-bristle brush or a Scotch-Brite scouring pad to texture the bases and break the suction against the snow.

Different temperatures of snow require different waxes. In the racing world there is a whole science to figuring out the fastest wax. For our purposes, it's best to rely on the block waxes you can buy at a ski shop. They have temperature charts on the back. If you're really confused, there are all-purpose waxes that work in all temperatures. You can also purchase a tin of rub-on wax for emergencies. This wax lasts only for a run or two, but it works fine if you don't have time for hot waxing, or between dates with the iron.

After your skis are tuned, store them using straps that separate the bases, to protect the freshly tuned bases and edges. You can buy straps with Velcro closures at any ski shop for $1 to $3.

Pack it up, store it right

Taking care of your equipment means packing and storing it so it lasts as long as possible. As with any sporting gear, there are ways to travel with gear and store it that will prevent damage.

A roof box is the best option for travel with skis because it offers the best protection.

Skis

To prevent damage to bases and edges from rust and other substances, store skis in a ski bag and keep them out of extreme temperatures or dampness. Just as water that gets into cracks in rocks expands when it freezes, the same process can affect the structure of the base of your skis. Before storing skis for long periods, hot wax the bases but don't scrape off the excess. This will provide an added layer of protection.

When traveling, hot wax the skis before leaving home and bring a scraper to prepare the bases just before you ski. This will keep the elements out while they ride on top of your vehicle or in the airplane. If you carry skis on top of your car, be sure to put them in a bag. The best way is to use a roof box that totally protects the whole ski, but at least cover the bindings to seal out road dirt and salt.

For airline travel, stuff some clothing around your skis inside their carrier to protect them as they are heaved from one baggage handler to another. Add some straps to the outside to keep them bundled tightly.

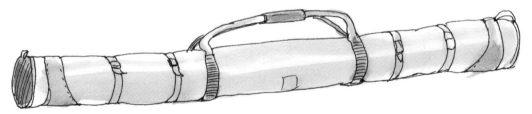

Bringing along your skis can actually provide more room for extra clothes in your ski bag!

Boots

The first line of defense in caring for boots is to be sure they dry out properly after each use. There are many gadgets on the market that will dry your liners overnight so moisture doesn't cause the material to deteriorate, making for cold feet. If you feel extravagant there are boot dryers that circulate air through your boot. The downside is that they may be noisy and keep you awake. My favorite device consists of small heating elements that plug into the wall. These elements never get hot enough to melt anything or burn you, but they'll dry your boots overnight. I especially like the price tag—about $25. Just remember to unplug them after twenty-four hours.

Once your boots are plugged in, be sure to fasten the buckles loosely. Plastic has a memory, and you may find yourself wrestling to close the top flap.

If you walk around much in your boots, consider purchasing a set of rubber boot sole covers. I use Cat Tracks, which slip onto the bottom of boots easily and prevent wear and tear, especially on heels. Worn boot soles can affect the binding release, so this is particularly important.

When storing boots for the summer, be sure all buckles are done up, and if possible keep them free of dust by placing them in a bag. Store them in a dry place away from extreme temperatures.

Taking care of your ski equipment keeps things functioning optimally, and it feels great to be in charge and know what has to be done and how. When you require the services of a ski shop, be sure you're in the driver's seat. Ask questions, and make sure you get what you pay for.

Top: This option is great when you're traveling.
Right: A traditional boot drying system.

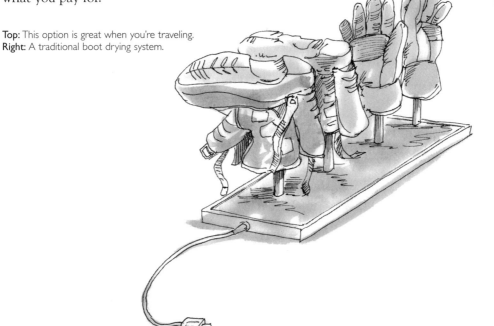

Chapter 8

FURTHER ADVENTURES

There are as many varieties of skiing as there are people who ski.

"The better you get, the better it gets!" This slogan says it all. Once you learn the basics, the options keep growing. There are as many varieties of skiing as there are people who ski. Find your style, practice with a pro, and turn up the fun meter. Here are some of the adventures you can choose from when you're ready.

RECREATIONAL RACING

Not every skier wants to race, but every racer needs to ski well. All racers can hone their technique and confidence by practicing on race courses, but race courses can also improve the technique of recreational skiers as well as provide fun and challenge.

Betsy began skiing later in life. She and her husband wanted a way to reunite family members who were leaving the nest by offering something fun to do and an occasion to get together in the winter. Betsy has trouble with her eyesight, causing her some anxiety while skiing. One day I asked her to ski through a race training course that I set for her. She was intimidated and immediately assumed she wasn't good enough, but with some encouragement she tried it.

That day was the biggest breakthrough in Betsy's skiing career. She cautiously negotiated

Mimi practices her racing skills.

SKIING RACE COURSES

Race training offers skiers many benefits:

- You learn to look farther ahead and plan tactics more quickly. This transfers to skiing in the woods, through moguls, and on narrow trails.

- Success in racing comes through limiting extra movements with the upper body and concentrating on the feet. This makes you more efficient and more likely to be comfortable on steep slopes or in varying conditions.

- A course dictates where you turn rather than allowing you to turn when you're ready. This is a confidence builder when the going gets tough.

- You learn to use the pole swing for rhythm and timing, a skill that is helpful on steeper slopes or in powder or bumps.

- Courses teach you to change direction earlier in the turn, which is necessary on steep, icy slopes.

the gates and was amazed to find that she focused so much on *where* to turn that *how* to turn became secondary. She began to look farther ahead and gain confidence that she could see what was coming. Later that day she brought her husband to a pay per run course (a race course open to the public at which you pay for each trip through the gates, usually $1) and challenged him to a race. She beat him! Ever since, she's felt able to try more trails and skis with confidence. Every once in a while they challenge the whole family to a friendly race, just to "stay sharp."

Friendly competition is an enjoyable way to stretch your skills, not to mention creating stories to share around the fireplace in the evening. Even relative beginners can find others at their skill level to challenge and share in the fun. Skiing a course can provide excitement if you're running out of challenges or if the weather is poor at the top.

. . . .

Friendly competition is an enjoyable way to stretch your skills, not to mention creating stories to share around the fireplace in the evening. Even relative beginners can find others at their skill level to challenge and share in the fun.

. . . .

Mogul competitions offer a fun and exciting way to practice your in-the-bumps skills.

••••••••••••••••••••••••••

There were competitors ranging from 8 to 68 years old, from just better than intermediate skiers to professional mogul champions.

••••••••••••••••••••••••••

You can find racing for recreational skiers at many resorts. It's worth taking a race clinic or lesson for learners, and many places offer group and private sessions. Other opportunities include coin-operated courses, competitions, and special "club" races sponsored by the resort for groups or ski clubs. Costs vary depending on the nature of the event.

MOGUL COMPETITIONS

Once you start having fun in the bumps (see pages 65–67), you might want to try a local mogul competition. These recreational events have been going on for quite some time. Many resorts hold them on special weekends in conjunction with parties, fireworks, or professional competitions.

The format varies, from dual elimination to solo performances. Usually a judge's stand is erected at the base of a particularly fun or challenging mogul run, the course is fenced off, and music is piped in. Competitors are judged on turns, jumps, and speed.

A couple of years ago I entered the "Bust 'n Burn" mogul competition at Sunday River, Maine's "Legends of Freestyle" event. It was such an exciting party that I wanted to be part of it. I woke up early the day of the event and went with friends to register. The schedule was simple. We could ski on the mogul course for the morning, practice the jumps (optional), and figure out our plan. There were competitors ranging from 8 to 68 years old, from just better than intermediate skiers to professional mogul champions. What made this competition even more fun was that the heroes of the early mogul competition days were competing against each other in the finals. Such legendary names as Scott Brooksbank and Wayne Wong skied head-to-head for bragging rights.

As I stood in the starting gate, adrenaline pumping, I was barely able to hear the music blaring from the loudspeakers over the thumping of my heart. I looked down the course and began to get butterflies. Then I looked over at the woman in the other starting gate and we both smiled. Suddenly we were just skiing again, and I could hear the music. When I completed the course, jumps and all, I was relieved to be still standing! My legs were shaking and I didn't win, but I was part of it all.

EXTREME SKIING

In extreme skiing skiers go off the beaten path to mountains without lifts or trails and ski steep faces—sometimes negotiating cliffs or rocks. The snow can range from lovely powder to coarse spring corn snow, slush that has been frozen, and everything in between. You usually reach these slopes by hiking at least part of the way. It's more wonderful because most skiers will never venture there. There are even competitions to see who can be the most daring and make the most dangerous lines look easy.

There are places where mere mortals can taste the "extreme" world and live to tell about it. Each spring groups of stalwart skiers make the trek up Mount Washington in New Hampshire into Tuckerman's Ravine. After about an hour's hiking you reach the base of the bowl. Then begins a steep climb that is hands over feet, the skis on your shoulder touching the wall of snow you're climbing. At first turning is difficult, since the steepness of the slope makes you catch your breath, but once you're in motion it becomes easy as gravity pulls you into each new turn. At the bottom, breathing once more, you look around and drink in the beauty of the place. If you happen to fall and slide a bit, you're cheered up by the folks eating lunch on the rocks at the base. That's enough to encourage any would-be extreme skier to continue.

The wilderness is anywhere you are that they aren't.

Even a series of turns in the trees can feel "extreme" if you're used to trails.

Should you dare to venture off the beaten path, prepare as if you're going on a wilderness hike. Remember, the wilderness is anywhere *you* are that *they* aren't. Bring plenty of water, clothing, maps, and first-aid supplies. Beware of avalanche danger, and if you're new to the sport, go with a guide.

The author reaps the rewards of her hike into the woods.

TREE SKIING

When the trails get crowded or there's a fresh fall of new snow, skiing in the woods is a great adventure. Trees add challenge yet provide a natural backdrop. Many resorts offer glades where the trees have been thinned out to make skiing between them easier. Even some beginner slopes offer such areas so learners can experience skiing in the woods.

Venturing into the trees can be intimidating if you look at all those solid bark-encrusted structures. In fact, looking at the trees can be hazardous. Instead, look for inviting paths between them. Planning your turns between the trees will help you focus on where you're going instead of on what you have to avoid. Once you learn to look ahead this way, pathways open up and you can create your own trail and your own adventure, run after run. Be sure to wear a helmet if you're headed into the trees.

NIGHT SKIING

Going at night makes skiing accessible to many city dwellers, especially during the week, and many resorts offer multiple-day lesson packages in the evenings. These programs are great for those who want to get in shape before a ski vacation at a larger resort.

Sometimes destination resorts offer night skiing on some of the terrain, which expands your options for ski time. Often other events at night lend a party atmosphere, such as snow tubing, recreational racing, torchlight parades, and fireworks.

Dress warmly when skiing at night, since the temperature often drops considerably. Also, wear goggles with clear lenses; dark daytime lenses can make it hard to see variations in the snow. Be sure to stay on trails that are well lighted. Terrain changes and obstacles can be hidden in shadows.

IN PURSUIT OF POWDER

Often referred to as the "ultimate" in skiing, powder snow can become a quest for "ski bums," who move from resort to resort, east to west, mountain range to mountain range looking for the stuff. When you experience your first turns in soft, bottomless snow, you'll understand. Making rhyth-

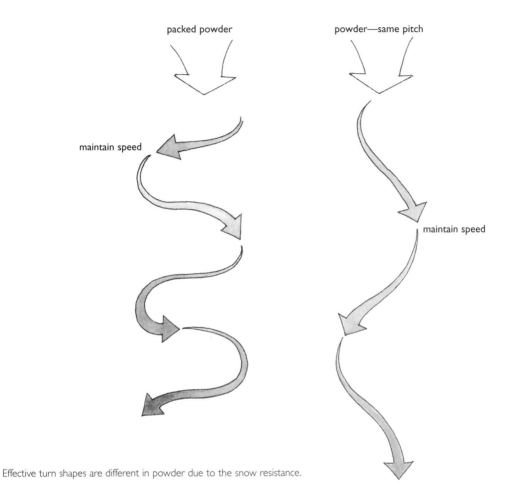

packed powder

powder—same pitch

maintain speed

maintain speed

Effective turn shapes are different in powder due to the snow resistance.

mic turns, floating down the hillside on a wave of soft white feathers, you feel as if you're in a cocoon. Your senses are heightened, and the exhilaration is indescribable.

Once a skier experiences this sensation, it can become addicting. Many skiers spend vacations heliskiing (helicopter skiing) or going into the back country on snowmobiles looking for the ultimate powder run. These adventures are expensive, yet they're well worth the cost if powder is what you crave.

Powder skiing can be captured at resorts as well. I've skied many exceptional powder days at both eastern and western resorts. The trick is to hit them either during or after a snowfall. Low temperatures and low humidity create light, fluffy snow that is delightful to ski in. The lighter the snow, the more desirable.

When powder is the condition of the day, head for steeper slopes and be prepared to ski faster than you normally would. Because of the greater resistance of the snow, more speed makes turning easier. Establish a good rhythm from turn to turn and stay centered over the middle of your skis. If

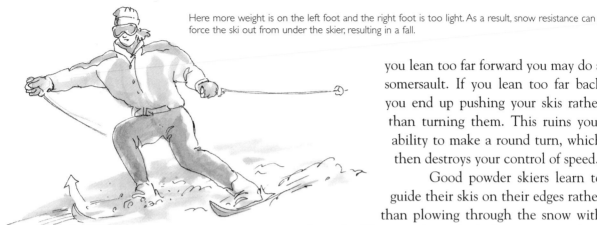

Here more weight is on the left foot and the right foot is too light. As a result, snow resistance can force the ski out from under the skier, resulting in a fall.

you lean too far forward you may do a somersault. If you lean too far back you end up pushing your skis rather than turning them. This ruins your ability to make a round turn, which then destroys your control of speed.

Good powder skiers learn to guide their skis on their edges rather than plowing through the snow with them flat. Keep weight on both skis; resistance from the snow can pull a ski out from under you and make you fall. Keep your ankles firm and "pull" your feet through the snow.

A tool for mastering powder more quickly is the "fat" ski, designed especially to help skiers float in the snow. Their buoyancy means these wide skis take less energy to turn. If you're new to powder and it's deeper than the top of your boots, try a pair.

Finally, to ski powder well and enjoy it to the point of addiction, be patient and find a rhythm. Watch videos of powder skiing and pay attention to the flow of the dance. Then give it a try.

The best part about skiing is that the adventure never stops. One trip to Disneyland and you've pretty much done it until they build a new attraction. At a ski resort the fun keeps on happening, no matter how many times you go. Although you don't have to be an expert to have a terrific time, as you play you also get better. And the better you get, the more adventures become available to you. There are some places in this world that only skiers can go. The rest of the world will never understand their allure.

The author and friends at the top of the world!

Chapter 9

BOOKS

This list of books is by no means exhaustive, but it covers the gamut: mind, spirit, technical, and women's issues.

Carbone, Claudia, *Women Ski*. Boston: World Leisure, 1996.

Mackenzie, Marlin. *Skiing; The Mind Game*. New York: Bantam Doubleday, 1993.

McNeil, Craig. *How to Ski the Blues and Blacks (Without Getting Black and Blue)*. Littleton CO: Blue Willow, 1998.

Milman, Dan. *The Warrior Athlete: Body, Mind, and Spirit*. Walpole NH: Stillpoint, 1979.

Post Foster, Ellen. *Racing Skills for Alpine Skiing*. South Hero VT: Turning Point Ski Foundation, 1994.

Post Foster, Ellen. *Skiing and the Art of Carving*. Edwards CO: Turning Point Ski Foundation, 1998.

Tejada-Flores, Lito. *Breakthrough on Skis*. New York: Vintage, 1986.

MAGAZINES

Inside Tracks
481 Sandy Point Ave.
Portsmouth RI 02871
401-846-7443
E-mail: ITracks@aol.com
This is really more like a monthly newsletter. It covers the latest and greatest, and helps uncover what works, where to find the best value, and even how to do it yourself!

Ski Magazine
Skiing Magazine
Skiing for Women (one issue a season)
Skiing Trade News
929 Pearl St., Suite 200
Boulder CO 80302
800-678-0871
http://www.skinet.com

VIDEOS

A lot of videos are out there, but here are a couple that really make a difference.

Breakthrough on Skis, vol. 1, *How to Get Out of the Intermediate Rut*. 58 min., Western Eye Productions, 800-333-5178.

Breakthrough on Skis, vol. 2, *Bumps and Powder*. 58 min., Western Eye Productions, 800-333-5178.

INFLEX
Adrian Crook's program is designed to increase your range of motion and maximize your movement for sport. Adrian Cook, P.O. Box 3519, San Clemente CA 92674-3519, 800-463-5393.

Mogul Mastery with Nelson Carmichael. 60 min., Freestyle Productions, 509-443-2272.

WEBSITES

These sites will help you link to everything from information on where to go to what to bring and where to shop. You can even purchase things over the Internet, if you choose! The best thing about using these sites is that you can check things out (even snow conditions by photograph) from the comfort of your living room.
http://www.iski.com
http://www.skinet.com
http://www.snowlink.com
http://www.rsn.com
http://www.aminews.com
http://www.snocountry.com
http://www.snowsportsresource.org
http://www.nsaa.org
http://www.psia.org

ORGANIZATIONS

National Ski Areas Association
133 South Van Gordon Street, Suite 300
Lakewood CO 80228
303-987-1111
Fax 303-986-2345
This is a consortium of ski resorts nation wide. They compile useful statistical information, and can be a resource for travel and regional information as well. (See the website listed above.)

Professional Ski Instructors of America
133 South Van Gordon Street, Suite 300
Lakewood CO 80228
303-987-9390
Fax 800-222-4754
A resource for all learners, this organization certifies the professionals who teach people to ski. (See the website listed above.)

Snow Sports Association for Women
A nonprofit organization founded in 1996, SSAW stays true to its mission to be the catalyst for expanding women's involvement in all snow sports. For information contact Jan Berg, Jberg@aol.com or Ingrid Niehaus, YWUK28A@ Prodigy.com.

Snow Sports Industries Association
This manufacturers group compiles information and resources for the equipment and clothing necessary to the sport. (See *<http://www.snowlink.com.>*.)

EQUIPMENT MANUFACTURERS

Following are the ski, boot, and binding companies featured in this book.

Skis, Boots, and Bindings

Elan
208 Flynn Ave., Box 4279
Burlington VT 05406
800-950-8900
http://www.elanskis.com

Marker, USA
1070 West 2300 South
Salt Lake City UT 84119
800-453-3862
http://www.markeri.com

Rossignol
P.O. Box 298
Williston VT 05495
802-863-2511
http://www.rossignol.com

Salomon North America
400 East Main St.
Georgetown MA 01833
800-225-6850
http://www.salomonsports.com

Technica USA
Volkl Sport America
19 Technology Drive
West Lebanon NH 03784
800-264-4579
http://www.volkl.com
http://www.technicausa.com

Accessories

Air Dry Systems
P.O. Box 88
Broomfield CO 80038-0088
800-237-6779
Boot-drying systems and boot heaters.

Boeri Helmets–MPH Associates, Inc.
Building 52, 61 Endicott St.
P.O. Box 567
Norwood MA 02062
781-555-9933

Bollé
Bollé America
3890 Elm St.
Denver CO 80207
800-628-2740

Briko/Luxoticca Group
44 Harbor Park Dr.
Port Washington NY
800-462-7456

Etc.
4600 Danvers Drive SE
Grand Rapids, MI 49512
800-423-1233
Grabber Warmers, disposable hand and boot warmers.

Leki USA, Inc.
356 Sonwil Drive
Buffalo NY 14225
800-225-9982
Poles.

Revo, Inc.
1315 Chesapeake Terrace
Sunnyvale CA 94089
800-843-7386
http://www.revo.com

Scott USA
P.O. Box 2030
Sun Valley ID 83353
800-292-5874
http://www.scottusa.com

Smartwool
E-mail: info@smartwool.com
Socks, underwear, gloves, headwear.

Smith Sport Optics
P.O. Box 2999
Ketchum ID 83340
208-726-4477

Swany America
Crossroads Industrial Park
Gloversville NY 12078
800-237-9269
http://www.swanyamerica.com
Gloves.

Uvex Sports
910 Douglas Pike
Smithfield RI 02917
888-616-8839
http://www.uvex.com

Tuning Equipment

FK Ski Tuning Tools
Ruffolo Enterprises
P.O. Box 597
Kenosha WI 53141
800-877-7025

Ski Visions
Reliable Racing
643 Upper Glen St.
Queensbury NY 12804
800-223-4448

Spiracut Sharptools
P.O. Box 3430
Hailey ID 83333
800-621-1657

CLOTHING MANUFACTURERS AND RETAILERS

Most brands can be found easily in retail shops.

Couloir USA, Inc.
732 Addison St., Suite C
Berkeley CA 94107
510-649-0852
http://www.couloir.com

Hard Corps Sports
P.O. Box 18330
Boulder, CO 80305
303-926-6750
http://www.hardcorps.com

Mountain Zone Marketplace
c/o The Zone Network
1415 Western Ave., Suite 300
Seattle WA 98101
206-621-8630
http://www.mountainzone.com

North Face
800-644-5232
http://www.thenorthface.com

Obermeyer
115 A.A.B.C.
Aspen CO 81611
800-525-4203
http://www.obermeyer.com

Patagonia Mail Order, Inc.
8550 White Fir Street
P.O. Box 32050
Reno NV 89533-2050
800-638-6464
http://www.patagonia.com

Spyder Active Sports, Inc.
3600 Pearl St.
Boulder CO 80301
E-mail: spyder-info@spyder.com

Title 9 Sports
Women's Sport Clothing
5743 Landregan Street
Emeryville CA 94608
510-653-9949
http://www.title9sports.com

Turtle Fur Company
P.O. Box 1010
Lamoille Industrial Park
Morrisville VT 05661-1010
800-52-NECKS
Neck gaiters and more.

RESORT INFORMATION

The best way to find out about resorts is to log onto one of the websites listed above. Here are some "women-friendly" resorts featuring programs for women.

California

Mammoth Mountain
760-934-2571
Reservations: 760-934-2581
Women's ski seminar, three-day programs.

Northstar at Tahoe
530-562-1010
Reservations: 800-GO-NORTH
Women's three-day workshop to improve technique, style, and confidence.

Squaw Valley
530-583-6965
Reservations: 800-545-4350
Women's clinics: three-day clinics with women instructors to increase skills and enjoyment of the sport.

Colorado

Aspen/Snowmass
970-925-1220
Reservations: 800-262-7736
Aspen Women's Weekend.

Crested Butte
970-349-2333
Reservations: 800-544-8448
Kim Reichhelm's Ski Adventures All-inclusive instructional ski vacations designed for women of all skiing abilities.

Steamboat
970-879-6111, ext. 531
E-mail: steamboat-info@
   steamboat-ski.com
Specialty women's weeks and workshops.

Telluride
970-728-6900
Reservations: 88-TELLURIDE
Women's weeks: four- and five-day programs.

Winter Park
970-726-5514
Reservations: 800-453-2525
Clinics, lessons, and programs specially designed for women, taught by women.

Maine

Sugarloaf, USA
207-237-2000
Reservations: 800-THE.LOAF
E-mail: info@sugarloaf.com
Women's Turn offers two- or three-day specialty programs.

Sunday River
207-824-3000
Reservations: 800-543-2SKI
E-mail: snowtalk@
   sundayriver.com
Women's Turn offers two- or three-day specialty programs, and a seasonal weekend program.

Massachusetts

Jiminy Peak
413-738-5500
Reservations: 800-882-8859
Women's Winter Escape every Tuesday and Wednesday; Ladies' Twilight/Night every Saturday.

Michigan

Crystal Mountain
616-378-2000
Reservations: 800-968-7686
Wednesday is Ladies Day.

Minnesota

Powder Ridge Ski and Snowboard Area
320-398-7200
Reservations: 320-398-7200
Thursday is Ladies Day during January and February.

Nevada

Heavenly
775-586-7000
Reservations: 800-2HEAVEN
Women's weeks.

New Hampshire

Attitash
603-374-2368
Reservations: 800-223-7669
E-Mail: info@attitash.com
Women's Turn workshops.

Loon Mountain
603-745-8111
Reservations: 800-229-LOON
Women's workshops available.

New Mexico

Taos Ski Valley
505-776-2291
Reservations: 800-776-1111
Women's Ski Weeks, Women's Weekends.

New York

Ski Windham
518-734-4300
Reservations: 800-729-4766
E-mail: skiwindm@aol.com
Inside Tracks Ski Program, by
reservation only.

Oregon

Mt. Ashland
541-482-2897
Reservations: 541-482-2897
Ladies Day on Wednesday; three-
day workshops for women.

Pennsylvania

Big Boulder
570-722-0100
Reservations: 800-468-2442
Women's Seminar is a compre-
hensive two-day program for all
abilities.

Blue Mountain
610-826-7700
Reservations: 610-826-7700
Women's Workshop meets on
Wednesdays for six weeks.

Jack Frost
570-443-8425
Reservations: 800-468-2442
Women's Seminar is a compre-
hensive two-day program for all
abilities.

Utah

Deer Valley
435-649-1000
Reservations: 800-558-3337
Women's Winter Escapes, Women
on Wednesdays, Women's
Weekend.

Park City Mountain Resort
435-649-8111
Reservations: 800-222-PARK
Women's Challenge Camps.

The Canyons
435-649-5400
Reservations: 888-CANYONS
Women's Turn offers two- or
three-day specialty programs.

Vermont

Bromley
802-824-5522
Reservations: 800-722-2159
Women's Mountain Experience
for skiers and snowboarders from
intermediate to expert.

Killington Resort/Pico Mountain
802-422-3333
Reservations: 800-621-MTNS
E-mail: info@killington.com
Women's Turn offers two- or
three-day specialty programs.

Mount Snow/Haystack
Reservations: 800-245-SNOW
E-mail: mtsno@sover.net
Women's Turn offers two- or
three-day specialty programs.

Okemo Mountain Resort
802-228-4041
Reservations: 802-228-5571
Women's weeks.

Sugarbush Resort
802-583-6310
E-mail: info@sugarbush.com
Women's Ski Escape offers two- or
three-day specialty programs.

SHOP INFORMATION

Ski shops are too numerous to
mention here. Ask a trusted friend
where to go, or get a recommen-
dation from your ski professional.
Barring that, log onto a website
listed above for listings of shops
and information about equipment
and clothing purchases.

Index